Landscape
DOCTOR

I dedicate this endeavor to my husband, Chris.
Without him, my knowledge and my life would be incomplete.

Landscape
DOCTOR

*Do-it-yourself remedies for
home planting problems*

By Sara Jane von Trapp

ILLUSTRATIONS BY KATHLEEN KOLB

CHAPTERS™

CHAPTERS PUBLISHING LTD., SHELBURNE, VERMONT 05482

Published by
Chapters Publishing Ltd.
2031 Shelburne Road
Shelburne, Vermont 05482

Library of Congress Cataloging-in-Publication Data
von Trapp, Sara Jane.
    Landscape doctor: do-it-yourself remedies for home planting problems /
by Sara Jane von Trapp; illustrated by Kathleen Kolb.
        p.   cm.
    Includes index.
    ISBN 1-881527-38-7: $29.95. — ISBN 1-881527-39-5: $19.95
    1. Landscape gardening. I. Title.
SB473.V66   1994
712'.6—dc20   94-27431

Trade distribution by
Firefly Books Ltd.
250 Sparks Avenue
Willowdale, Ontario
Canada M2H 2S4

Printed and bound in Canada by
Metropole Litho
St. Bruno de Montarville, Quebec

Designed by Susan McClellan
Cover illustration by Kathleen Kolb

Photography Credits
Richard W. Brown: pages 48-49; 88.
Gary Clayton-Hall: pages 8-9; 39; 66-67; 78-79.
Jerry Pavia: pages 110-111; 130.

Contents

Introduction

MY GRANDMOTHER CAREFULLY CROSS-STITCHED AND FRAMED the following words, which went on the wall in my bedroom where I have read them just before falling asleep every night since I learned to read:

"Your garden is God's gift to thee: Thus sing the birds from every tree."

Looking back, I wonder if there wasn't something prophetic in my grandmother's handiwork. It would have saved a lot of floundering around in college if I had realized from the start that I was destined to enter the planting profession.

For the past fifteen years, I have been a professional landscaper and co-owner of a tree nursery. Early on, I began to notice that despite the vast differences in the scope of my jobs—everything from flat suburban postage-stamp lots to sweeping estates of lakeshore and mountainside—I was encountering the same basic landscaping problems over and over again. Although the homes I have landscaped have ranged from the ultra-modern to two-century-old Federalist, and the budgets of clients from hundreds of dollars to tens of thousands, no one was immune to problems such as improper grading, too much foundation show, obtrusive utility boxes and wet and shady planting sites.

Over time, I began to view myself as something of a landscape doctor, experienced at curing these and other common landscaping ills. Physicians may disagree, but I believe that as a landscaper, I am asked more than other professionals for advice, no matter where I am or what context it is in. Like medical doctors, I've usually heard the questions before. This book is my way of putting the answers on paper.

The advice on the following pages is based on my real experience so the homeowner can avoid the pitfalls of blind encounters. My advice is also based on years of working with do-it-yourself clients to develop easily understandable methods that can be realized without hiring so-called experts. Most of the tasks that I suggest can be done economically and enjoyably by anyone who has a few weekend days to spend in the yard.

Landscaping is a highly rewarding pursuit, which is probably why I consider it my avocation as well as my profession. I put up with the whims of nature, pestilence and adverse weather, all for the love and thrill of working outdoors and witnessing life in its purest form. Because I live in a four-season climate, my juices start to flow along with the budding trees and emerging crocuses in the spring. I am fully and absolutely influenced by the recurrent rituals of plant life. That is why I continue to do what I do, and why this book was written.

—Sara Jane von Trapp

Acknowledgments

MANY INDIVIDUALS HAVE SHOWN INTEREST, provided encouragement and given solid advice as this project moved towards fruition. A few must be singled out for their memorable contributions.

First, thank you to my good friends Alice Lawrence, for helping me plant the seed, and James Lawrence, for letting it grow. My editor, Barry Estabrook, was instrumental in causing it to flourish and mature. Susan McClellan was responsible for the remarkable flowing design, and illustrator Kathleen Kolb was a gem. This was not an easy task, but she met adversity head on and produced outstanding results.

Many thanks to Norm Pellett, friend and professor of Ornamental Horticulture at the University of Vermont, for his ready answers, to Leonard Perry, extension agent, and Dr. Richard Klein, retired professor of Botany at the University of Vermont, for being important resources.

Recognition is due my colleagues and fellow New England Nursery Association Board Members, past and present, especially Fred Dabney, Frank Thomann, Neal Millane, Dale Pierson and Tommy Vanicek for giving me the honor of first woman president, which greatly bolstered my self-confidence, helping to make this book possible.

My appreciation to a dear friend, Teena Flood, who helped in the early stages to make my writing homeowner friendly. Thanks to my mother-in-law, Henriette von Trapp, for such positive reinforcement along the way.

Special acknowledgment to my family: my parents, Nat and Edith Gould, for believing in me so deeply, my husband, Chris, for technical assistance and repeated encouragement, and to my children, Kate, Jakob and Rebecca, who gave up the computer and the TV on many occasions so Mom could write in peace.

Finally, I am also indebted to the many homeowners whose properties I had the privilege to work on. A special thank you to clients Skip and Ginny Farrell and Robert Hamilton, who have stood by us all these years.

Chapter One

THE
Front Entry

Practical & pleasing approaches

F I HAVE AN OBSESSION with front entries, I at least came by it honestly. For four years after we had "completed" our house, our front door hung at second-story level, eight feet above the ground, without landing or steps. The door was nailed shut to stop curious guests and toddlers bound for certain injury. With two young children to feed and shelter, my husband and I opted for a kitchen and insulation instead of the front entry. Our front door to nowhere was the result of a spent construction budget.

Eventually, the front entry did get completed. But the experience of those first four years has left me sensitive to front entry problems. Whether building costs are in the hundreds of thousands or tens of thousands, too often the plan for the front entry landscaping is altered or even abandoned until the homeowners recover from the costs of building. And even then, the front entry is often poorly or unimaginatively designed—an afterthought, in all ways.

This is unfortunate. Planning for the entry landscaping should be included as a comprehensive part of the house design. It is less expensive to integrate the grading, driveway, walkway and front door in one design than to augment the plan later.

When considering the front entry for a new house or fixing a poorly planned existing one, it is important to begin by examining the essential elements that comprise a well-arranged entry. They include an inviting approach, a safe, easy-to-negotiate walkway and steps and a proper lighting scheme, all incorporated into a visually desirable plan. Scrimping on entry landscaping is

not always necessary, especially when the entry area can be designed and installed by the homeowner and phased in, over time, at considerable savings.

E.B. White, in *Elements of Style*, said it best: "Design informs even the simplest structure, whether of brick-and-steel or of prose. You raise a pup tent from one vision, a cathedral from another. This does not mean that you must sit with a blueprint always in front of you, merely that you had best anticipate what you are getting into."

Best Laid Plans

D ESIGNING THE FRONT ENTRY need not be intimidating. The best way to begin is to sit with a piece of graph paper and sketch the front wall of your house accurately to scale as a bird's-eye view. Then indicate the windows and door(s), and include any other structures in the front yard, as well as trees you want to keep because they provide shade in summer, wind protection, are a noise buffer or are simply pleasing to view.

Next, make a list of plants worth transplanting. Any thriving plant that is small enough to dig up easily while including a good

portion of roots may be salvageable. When deciding on the "keepers," remember to choose a properly exposed transplanting site compatible with the type of plant being saved; for example, a shade-loving plant should not be replanted in a sunny situation. Also, study the potential growth habit of the plant to be sure it won't become too large or the wrong shape for its planned spot. Any plant that is either overgrown or has one-sided foliage (because it was growing too close to another plant) or is unsuitable for the new site should be transplanted to the edge of the property or yanked and discarded if it is too far gone.

Leave the rest of the graph paper clean and ready for the new design. Be flexible in planning: almost anything can be moved, removed or camouflaged. Take the time to survey the entire yard objectively by stepping back from the house, even into the street or driveway or a neighboring yard, to look at the whole picture.

Some people need to view their design in three dimensions and find it easiest to use a prop like a rubber garden hose whose flexibility allows bending and shaping of the outline of the new walk or planting bed when it's laid out on the ground. String, stretched between stakes, may help in laying out the plan for a straight-edged

With thoughtful planning, an unimaginative front entry, **left,**
can be made pleasing and welcoming, **above.** *In the well-planned example,
notice how the sidewalk swings away from the house and approaches the door in a series of gentle
curves. These allow space for plantings that add texture and interest to the front
of the house, which appears plain and monotonous when
approached on a straight sidewalk.*

courtyard or entry deck. Be generous with space allotment in the design, if room allows. The approach and steps should be wide enough for two people to pass comfortably side by side (at least four feet wide). Even a cramped front yard will benefit from an inviting, broad walkway, if only achieved by creating an illusion of space through splaying the end of the walkway that merges with the driveway or sidewalk. Where space is ample, splaying the walkway ends makes a more natural, gentle meeting point at perpendicular junctions as well as conveying a warm invitation directing guests to the desired entry.

Form Follows Function

AS THE CONCEPTUAL PLAN DEVELOPS, it is important to consider function first, then how the layout can be more attractive. Essential aesthetic components like composition and balance are the foundation for a successful design.

To achieve balance, again step back and consider the whole picture. A tree or building on one side must have equal weight on the other, but not necessarily its exact counterpart. A single large, heavy object like a tree can be

When space allows, the ends of a sidewalk should be splayed where they join the driveway or intersecting walkways. In contrast to a hard, perpendicular intersection, splaying creates a more natural, gentle meeting point that conveys a warm invitation directing guests to the desired door.

In landscape design, balance is achieved when a tree or other object on one side of an entrance is matched with objects of equal weight on the other. But the two sides need not be mirror images. The two groups of shrubs on the right balance the larger group on the left.

balanced by several smaller objects or plants placed in a grouping. A front door can be framed on each side with identical plants, the so-called symmetrical approach. But it is also possible, and usually desirable, to attain aesthetic balance without symmetry. Balance through symmetry creates a formal look perfect for the Georgian or Federal-style home, while asymmetry is more casual and compatible with contemporary architecture. Whichever approach you choose, remember that

plants change shape and grow, which may throw off the balanced plan in a few years.

Once the basic spaces have been defined, color and texture, two remaining design essentials, are incorporated. Details such as walkway and step materials, plantings and lighting make the design unique and attractive.

After the basic components have been sketched onto the graph paper, it is time to move to the next step, engineering, so that the purchase of materials can be performed intelligently and economically. This requires measuring square footage, figuring a framing plan for wood projects and a game plan for the others, and listing all tools and materials needed.

The proper order for installation should now be considered. First, all the heavy excavation and moving of building materials and soil will be performed when you have a skid steer loader or other moving machine on site. Planning ahead will ensure that the equipment will not be needed later, after it has left. Next, start the part of the project closest to the house, working from the front door to the driveway or street, so that one piece of the plan won't be spoiled by having work done over it. By all means, leave the plantings until last so they won't be abused during construction.

Often, those first stages aren't the most attractive; sometimes they don't even seem noticeable, but a landscape project, carried out over seasons or years, will ultimately succeed because it has been designed as a whole. For me, there is nothing more satisfying than having a project finally come together. My own front door, which once plagued me with its lonely dominance, is now integrated as a part

of an overall design, making the entry warm and inviting. And it is no longer nailed shut.

Problem

Walkways:
Too Straight, Too Narrow

A FEW YEARS AGO, I visited a small urban yard and cottage that needed an entry to accommodate a new addition. Exactly where the entry should be was a huge oak tree dating from the Revolutionary War era. Every construction and landscaping decision was based on the root spread of that tree, its canopy and its trunk location. Creating a new entry with a direct route to the front door was out of the question because it would pile earth on top of the roots, which would slowly suffocate the majestic tree.

And it doesn't have to be a Revolutionary-era tree. A large rock, an outbuilding, a septic bed or a flower garden—all of these obstacles seem to take a perverse delight in standing in the way of a straight route to the front door. Perhaps they are trying to tell landscape designers something: while forging a direct route is both convenient and practical, it is more often than not the least aesthetic way to get where you want to go.

Remedy

Reroute It For
Design's Sake

EVEN IF IT ISN'T NECESSARY to skirt aged trees or other obstacles, giving shape to the walk—a gentle sweep or

In the example at left, the contractor has made the common mistake of running a sidewalk too close to the exterior wall of a house, thereby emphasizing the harsh meeting of two man-made objects. With a gently curving sidewalk placed well away from the wall, the hard, square lines of the same home become softened, **above**. *The extra space allows more room for plantings, further reducing the hard effect of the abrupt meeting of house and sidewalk.*

curve—softens the hard lines of the house walls and provides more space for planting.

It makes sense to leave an area for shrubs and flowers between the house and walkway. In addition to providing an accessible, highly visible place to put plants, it has the added ad-vantage of eliminating the harsh meeting of two man-made surfaces. Traversing a serpentine walkway gives people arriving at a house pause for appreciating various perspective views of the home. A curving walk also provides nooks for attractive plantings.

The Hidden Entry

I've FOUND THAT many homes today are built with the garage protruding out into the driveway. Often the overhead garage door is the most prominent feature. In many cases, the driveway approaches the garage from the side of the house, so that the location of the front entry—the one to which most homeowners want to steer guests—is hidden or awkward to approach.

I've also seen front entries tucked away in an inside corner where the garage wall meets the front wall of the house, leaving no area for plantings between the wall and the walk as well as obscuring the door. In such cases, when the plantings reach maturity, the front door becomes a cave opening in a jungle of foliage.

Another common entry problem is that two doors are sometimes built on the front face of the house, one for guests and the other for family. When confronted with more than one, I always opt for the larger, more prominent door and am often met with, "No one ever uses my front door!" Arriving at a party once, my husband and I followed another couple to the family door and were bullied by the hosts, who made us go to the guest door.

Emphasize the Correct Doors

As THE ABOVE EXAMPLES show, what door to use is not always clear. But you need not resort to bullying to clarify your desires. A few surprisingly simple landscaping sleights of hand can direct visi-

tors to the correct door. By building a large deck at the level of the door's threshold, the entry location is emphasized. Stretch the deck from the corner of the house to beyond the

Commonly, houses are built in such a way that guests are faced with making the choice between two doors on the same wall. The goal of the landscaper should be to maximize the effect of the primary entry by making it obvious and inviting. To emphasize main walks, they should be made wider (at least four and a half to five feet wide) than secondary walks.

door. Then, offset the steps or walk-on point of the deck to bring the walk away from the house.

If the door is hidden from the parking area, the deck should protrude into the yard far enough to catch the attention of visitors. That was an effective solution for the side entry of a small cottage a friend of mine designed. The guest door was on the far side of the house, well away from the parking area. One choice was to create a circular driveway that brought the door into view from the car. The yard was too small for so much driveway, but the deck, which was enclosed with half walls sheathed with the same siding as the house, created an additional outdoor living space with an inviting opening facing the front.

When there is a choice of two doors on one wall, maximize the primary entry by making it obvious and inviting. The main walk should

---

One of the most simple and effective ways to emphasize a front door is to enlarge the entry platform. In the example below, the deck extends from the corner of the house well beyond the door and far enough out into the yard to catch the attention of guests who would not be able to see the door itself from the parking area.

*Building a jog in a secondary walk as it leaves the main pathway
makes a mudroom entrance, such as the one above, less inviting to visitors who
might otherwise automatically choose the door that is closest to the parking area.
By forcing them out of their way, the jog signals that they should
continue on the main sidewalk to the front entrance.*

be wider (at least four and a half to five feet wide) than the one that leads to the secondary entryway. It should be uninterrupted and splayed where it meets the driveway or street. It is ideal to sweep it away from the house face enough so that visitors can get glimpses of the front door as they move along the walk.

By day, plantings that provide focal points along the path will lure the visitor to the correct door, especially if the plants are colorful or have interesting shapes. Warm-colored blossoms, reds and yellows, stand out and draw the eye, and small flowering trees like crab apples provide year-round interest with spring flowers, summer green, fall color, and fruits that persist into winter when naked branches and twigs show skeletal form and texture. Upright, prunable evergreens like yew, arborvitae or juniper are fine choices for accent plants as well. Highlighting those plantings at night similarly draws the visitor along the walkway.

Minimizing the secondary or family entry takes a little more imagination. In some cases, both walkways merge where they meet the driveway or street. Getting to the family entry requires a detour off the main path. Always make the secondary walkway narrower. Its visibility can be further reduced by making the surface material of the secondary walk different from that of the main walkway. Use smaller stone, a less intricate pattern in the pavers, or use rockfines (also known as stone-dust), a crushed stone that has the texture of very

coarse sand and becomes as firm as concrete after several wettings.

Strategically placed plants blocking the view to the secondary door will divert visitors from taking that path. Cool-colored plants recede from view, so use pastel blues and purples to adorn the mudroom walk. Building a jog in the walk as it leaves the main path will make the secondary walkway less inviting and force guests to make a concerted effort to go out of their way if they choose to use it.

When the two walks are separate at their origin, it is easy to minimize the secondary path. Simply hide the lesser path with an island of plants, which throws the main walkway into the line of sight as the house is approached. If there is limited space for the plantings, a narrow hedge of evergreens or thickly branched flowering shrubs or even windowsill-height fencing is effective. Beware the danger of introducing fencing or barriers too close to the house. Blend fencing into the surroundings by staining it the same color as the house, by repeating shapes and styles compatible with the house and by keeping it low enough to look appropriate. Planting on the street side of the fence will minimize its impact as well.

If the two entries are separated by a lot of space, if each has its own driveway or parking area or if the secondary door doesn't share the front of the house, there may be no confusion. Attractive plantings for daytime visitors and proper lighting by night will be enough to direct people to the entry of choice.

Problem

Slopes & Puddles

Walkways that have puddles or slippery, icy patches in winter are difficult and dangerous to negotiate. Even when the walkways are dry, bumps and holes make them treacherous. Too much slope in a walkway is also a nightmare during inclement weather. A slope can be slippery for an able-bodied person, but invite an elderly friend to dinner—or a family with young children—and you'll realize what a hardship such a walk can be.

Remedy
Proper Grading

Grade and drainage should be of primary concern and, properly executed, will solve most if not all puddling and settling problems. Water must be directed away from the entry area. For that reason, it is important to always grade away from the house. Allow at least one inch of pitch for every eight feet.

In most cases, steps will be a part of the front entry, especially if the alternative is a sloping walkway. They should be wide enough to accommodate two people side by side, and the treads should be generous enough in depth to lay an entire foot flat on them. Be careful in measuring treads that must be very deep: full-stride steps should be just that, full strides, even if there is more than one stride per tread. A half step is not only awkward but unsafe, especially after dark.

By the same token, the risers, or the vertical portions of steps, must not be too short or too tall, and they must be equal from stair to stair. The rule of thumb calls for outdoor risers between six and eight inches in height.

When engineering the stairs, use a transit, a hand-held or tripod-mounted device that determines grades. A transit will accurately indicate the difference between the top of the grade, which might be an existing landing, threshold or deck, and the bottom of the grade or level at which the stairs end. Once that difference has been determined, divide the total figure by the desired riser height to find out how many steps are needed. Riser height may need slight adjustments to make the steps equal and to make sure that all steps fall within the six- to eight-inch riser parameters.

Formidable numbers of steps are best divided into a series of landings and groupings of stairs. By making the climb more gradual, landings ease the strain for visitors carrying bundles and provide possibilities for design. The stairs may curve or wind and be constructed of interesting materials. They can also provide different levels for plantings or planter

boxes while giving access to the front door.

When steps must be a part of the front entry, integrate them well enough into the design so that they appear to be an intentional part of it, not just a necessary appendage.

Problem

Hard-to-Maintain Walkways

I ONCE HAD THE UNPLEASANT experience of rebuilding an entire front entry a year after it had been installed with "bad" stone. It looked as if someone had dropped a bomb on the rocks. Nearly all of the stones had shattered. Needless to say, it was a costly and discouraging affair. People are too often lured by the quaintness of old brick or the seeming practicality of reusing salvaged stone. Freezing and thawing fluctuations cause unsuitable stone and brick to crumble when moisture enters the pores or fissures, freezes, then expands.

Maintenance of natural stone can be a nuisance when the edges of the stone are caught with the snowshovel or shattered with a snowblower. Further, natural stone surfaces are, more often than not, uneven, and therefore

---

Steps should be wide enough to accommodate two people walking side by side. The stairs themselves should be deep enough for an entire foot, plus some, to lay flat on them. Risers should be between six and eight inches high. Formidable numbers of steps should be broken up by landings to make the climb more gradual. This has the added advantage of providing different levels for plantings.

treacherous for unsteady walkers: toddlers, the elderly or persons with disabilities.

Remedy
Choose the Right Surface

CONSIDERING THE EFFORT and expense invested in walkway installation, it is worth taking the time to explore the possibilities for walkway surfaces. Ease of maintenance should be an important factor, if not *the* most important, in the decision.

There are many types of surfaces available. Natural stones vary in their ability to withstand freezing and thawing, so seek the advice of someone familiar with the stone and local conditions before making your choice. Some stones split or plate easily. Avoid them at all costs. Similarly, chimney brick must not be used for walkways. The same goes for old brick salvaged from building projects. Paving bricks are more dense than standard house-construction bricks and are manufactured with additives to make them strong and weatherproof. Bluestone, a natural, flat-quarried, bluish-colored stone, is relatively easy to maintain and traverse.

Concrete is the easiest walkway surface with which to live, the most economical, and the best for withstanding abuse. Don't discount it out of hand for seemingly more attractive alternatives. I have seen many poured-concrete surfaces colored and stamped with patterns that add interest. Precast concrete pavers in various shapes and colors withstand weather and wear because of their density and configuration. Most shapes fit together tightly, discouraging weeds from growing between, and the beveled edges act as expansion joints in freezing weather. When properly manufactured, concrete pavers can withstand 5,000 pounds of pressure per square inch, which means they can be driven on, snowblown or plowed—like asphalt or poured concrete.

It is always worthwhile to explore the advantages and disadvantages of the various surface materials available for walkway construction. **From left to right:** *Carefully fitted together fieldstones are attractive, but they vary in their ability to withstand freezing and thawing. Precast-concrete pavers are available in many shapes, colors and sizes. Bluestone, a natural, flat-quarried, bluish-colored stone, is relatively easy to maintain.*

Problem
Unsightly Stoops & Steps

Ince rehabilitated the landscaping at a home that was formerly owned by a concrete contractor. He must have loved his work. The entire house was encircled with walkways more characteristic of city sidewalks than the quiet setting of his home.

Step One in my renovation plan was simple and straightforward: call in a skid steer loader. Ripping out that sidewalk was easy with the right machinery, and so satisfying.

The front entry is now expansive instead of defined by the sidewalks. The sweeping approach pulls the walkway away from the sides of the house, allowing for a large planting bed and a perspective that wasn't possible within the confines of the concrete sidewalk system.

Sometimes, the problem is not so easy to solve: when the existing front stoop can't be removed because it was poured as a part of the foundation walls, when an elderly parent joins the household and can't negotiate the stair arrangement, or when the shrubs in the front yard are so overgrown that the windows are obscured.

Remedy
Camouflage or Remove

Whatever the reason for rehabilitation, remember my motto: most anything can be moved, removed or camouflaged. This is particularly true for unsightly stoops and steps. First, decide which elements of the existing entry should be salvaged. Then, incorporate those features into the plan and work the other details around them. Saving certain plants or features may require tricky machine maneuvering so as not to harm or injure what's being saved, so decide if it is worth the time and expense to keep a shrub that may be easier, less expen-

---

*Brick, **left**, can make a walkway surface that is functional, but only if bricks specifically designed for paving are used. Paving bricks are more dense than house-construction bricks and are manufactured with additives to make them strong and weatherproof. **Below**, natural fieldstones placed some distance apart with grass allowed to grow between can make an effective walkway.*

*Almost any unsightly landscape feature can be moved, removed or—as illustrated above—
camouflaged. Here, a poured-concrete stoop has been completely hidden beneath a new cedar
entry deck, much more in keeping with the traditional look of the house's siding.*

sive or more attractive if replaced than worked around.

An immovable existing poured-concrete entry stoop can be covered with a wooden deck. One entry I designed had a front door moved to accommodate an expanded kitchen. The existing stoop was no longer in sync with the door and no longer the right width because the front door was now way off-center. A cedar entry deck was constructed to match the new siding and covered the poured-concrete deck.

Alternatively, it is possible to "face" (a method of masonry appliqué) a concrete pad with a natural stone product like bluestone or with half-thickness paving bricks, a common product found at masonry suppliers. Facing with a new material is a simple way of achieving a fresh look. It can also be a way to bridge old parts of a house with new additions. When a friend put an addition on her house, she faced the existing concrete stoop with blue-stone to blend with the style of the addition. It was a less expensive alternative to removing the existing stoop and starting over.

Too Many Steps:

I T IS NOT UNUSUAL for the front yard to be higher than the driveway, requiring a number of steps to reach the entry door.

A common problem in many front yards—and a virtual certainty with split-level ranches—too many steps between the driveway and the front door can be a major inconvenience. Instead of a straight up-and-down staircase, consider a timber planter/stair system.

Most prevalent with a split-level ranch house where the door is midway between the basement and the first floor level, fifteen or so steps required in a short distance may make the weary homeowner or visitor wish for an escalator. Finding new ways to approach the door is a test of the imagination.

Remedy
Multi-Level Systems

A MULTITUDE OF STAIRS can pose a problem. But stairs can also present opportunities for interesting design that, at the same time, can reduce the fatigue of climbing. The key for turning this problem into an opportunity is to break up flights of stairs with frequent landings. Instead of a straight up-and-down staircase, consider some variations involving a timber planter/stair system that creates several shallow boxes, space for perennial plants and shrubs. If shallowly built, the boxed planters do not extend out of the ground far enough to threaten freezing of the roots. The wooden stair complexes wind towards the entry and eliminate the need for steps out the front door.

Rather than approaching the house from below the entry, the user meets the door at its level, which gives a full perspective view of the house, usually difficult to achieve with some modern house designs, particularly the ubiquitous split-level ranch.

To eliminate mowing the slope to the driveway, a stepped retaining wall can be built the full length of the drive, tying into an entry system that extends past the door across the house. That creates a level of planter equal in height to the door, giving dimension to the house face and widening the entry stoop. By incorporating uncommon landscape design and techniques, the most common architectural style becomes refreshing.

Problem
Inadequate Nighttime Lighting

EVEN MY FATHER, who, over time, has come to respect his daughter's opinion—at least on matters related to landscaping—still does not understand that floodlights attached to a building are not only blinding, but are actually an advantage to a burglar because they shine the light away from the house and create a shadow precisely where the burglar wants to lurk: by your door or window. Safety lighting should always shine towards the home.

Virtually every traditional way of providing outdoor lighting is impractical and only of ornamental value. Carriage lights attached to a wall like sconces do not project light. A lamp on a post at the end of the walk is decorative by day, but relatively useless at night because it is at blinding eye level.

Remedy
A Proper Lighting Scheme

WHEN DESIGNING the landscaping for a new home, include a lighting plan, because wiring should be installed at the outset of the project regardless of when the fixtures are installed. That said, improvements in low-voltage systems have made retrofitting existing homes much easier than it

Low-voltage lighting has made retrofitting ineffective home-lighting systems much simpler than it was even a few years ago. In addition to being practical, low-voltage lights can also be used to create aesthetic effects with the subtle interplay of light and shadow. **Above,** *back lighting makes a shrub near the front entry a nighttime focal point.*

used to be, even a few years ago. I am a proponent of the low-voltage variety because of its versatility, easy installation, and comparatively (to conventional voltage) inexpensive fixtures.

A well-planned front entry puts the task lighting at your feet, where it's needed. Proper lighting will direct guests to the right door

and, conversely, by its absence, cause them to avoid a mudroom entrance.

Old myths perpetuating the inadequacies of dim low-voltage lighting just do not hold true. If you still subscribe, consider that automobile headlamps are low-voltage. Dimness is a factor of poor installation and occurs when

*A well-planned lighting scheme for the front entry has to accomplish
several tasks at one time. Low-to-the ground fixtures direct light to where it is
needed—at guests' feet—and away from their eyes, where it would only blind them.
At the same time, proper lighting leads visitors to the right door. Through the techniques
of uplighting and downlighting, inconspicuous fixtures highlight the branching habits
and bark of shrubs and trees, providing nighttime focal points
and drawing visitors toward the entrance.*

wires are overtaxed with too many fixtures or when the wrong size transformer is used.

EVEN THOUGH THERE ARE MANY lovely looking light fixtures on the market, I prefer the light itself and the different effects one can create with it. Low-voltage lighting fixtures are primarily inconspicuous. It is the light they shed that catches attention. Uplighting or downlighting on trees and shrubs highlights branching habits and provides nighttime focal points, drawing visitors to the door. The same can be accomplished with backlighting, which also creates wonderful shadows on walls. Periodic placement of light fixtures along a walkway low to the ground is perfectly adequate for most applications. How far apart the lights are placed or how many lights are needed is dictated by the type of fixture and bulb used.

Another advantage of low-voltage lighting is that the homeowner is able to install it. Once an electrician has provided a conventional 120-voltage line, anyone can attach a transformer to it. A transformer is a small box that changes the voltage and can be installed inside or out, depending on the type purchased. I have even buried a "raintight" transformer in the ground in a plastic box normally used for a lawn-sprinkler installation. Transformers are easily hidden with shrubs or in a garage or shed. Wires leading from low-voltage transformers to fixtures may be buried as shallowly as desired in the ground or under mulch.

THE NUMBER OF FIXTURES you can use is dictated by the size of the transformer and the voltage of the bulbs. Usually, fixtures are placed in the ground on a spike that allows the flexibility of moving them as long as some slack is left in the wire. More fixtures can be added later if the transformer is large enough, a versatile advantage for growing trees and shrubs or a phased-in landscape plan.

In order to make final adjustments to the fixtures once they are installed, it is necessary to wait until dusk or later. My husband, Chris, has been known to curse lighting (and me) because it forces us to work late into the night, especially during the summer, when it doesn't get dark until nine o'clock. Chris would agree that we've had some of our best arguments with him teetering at the top of the ladder wielding a light fixture while I point my finger . . . a little to the left . . . a little to the right. But after he's come down off the ladder and had a chance to view the results, he generally agrees the effort was worthwhile.

Although some low-voltage fixtures are made of expensive metals like brass or copper, I recommend aluminum, which is usually painted black or green and is both less expensive and less obtrusive.

Whether opting for regular or low-voltage lighting, avoid eye-level placement and resist overdoing it. Leave that spectacle for parking lots and shopping malls. For design's sake, there is much to be said for the subtle interplay of shadow and light, and while low-voltage lighting is quite task-effective, it is its subtlety that I find so appealing.

Although it may sound like sacrilege to anyone who has planted and nursed along
young shrubs, those little plants can grow to a point where they threaten to become unsightly
obstacles. In this home, the evergreens now cover many of the windows and even block one
doorway. They also effectively screen the view of the front door from the driveway.
The illustration on page 35 shows the same home with a refurbished front entry.

Problem

Overgrown & Overplanted

To anyone who has planted and then nursed along young shrubs it inevitably sounds like sacrilege, but the fact is that those little plants can grow to the point where they completely obscure the front entry, sending the signal "Do not enter." Some trees and shrubs can very effectively block the way, which, unless it's intentional, keeps a guest from using the right door. After a number of years, that sapling grows up to be the tree it was supposed to, now unsightly and an obstacle. People also tend to have an attachment to their plants much as they do to their pets, and they grow so used to the way the plants and house look, it's often difficult to make a change.

Remedy

Prune or Remove

Pruning or removing overgrown shrubs is one of the quickest and least expensive ways to rehabilitate the front entry. Some gardeners also find it downright cathartic. Like the rest of nature, plants have a lifespan and outgrow their usefulness if pests don't cause their demise first. A good example involves one of my favorite plants, daphne

'Carol Mackie'. It is a very hardy, scented, spring-flowering shrub with striking, variegated leaves. A friend of mine who grows 'Carol Mackie' calls it the "seven-year shrub." Unfortunately, nature has provided it with a growth habit that causes some of the branches to break where they meet the main stem as it gets larger. No amount of pruning, however judicious, stops the bacterial blight that enters at the breaks. There is no effective cure or prevention for this bacterial disease. 'Carol Mackie' is such a beautiful plant that it is worth enjoying for its seven years or so, but it eventually needs to be replaced.

OTHER SHORT-LIVED PLANTS like gray birch, silver maple, Lombardy poplar, and Russian olive are popular because they grow so fast, making "instant" windbreaks and screens between neighboring yards. Storms and wind do them in eventually. In nature, many of these trees are succession plants that fill the space between an old field or meadow and a hardwood forest. It is prudent to plant less rapid growers that are notoriously long-lived along with trees with shorter lifespans so that, when the time comes to remove them, the stable plants will be established enough to fill the space.

Older varieties of deciduous shrubs like forsythia, spiraea and lilac, if left to their own devices for years, will eventually become less floriferous, too large for their home in the landscape, and less desirable than their newly developed dwarf and improved counterparts. The old-fashioned bridalwreath spiraea, for example, has superior new cousins that are more compact in growth habit, bloom more vigorously and hold more usefulness for a front entry planting because of their smaller mature size. Plants like lilacs, forsythia and yews should be removed if regular maintenance has not been done, if a plant is broken or thinly branched or if too many plants were originally put too close together.

Naturally, most plants will have a longer lifespan if maintained properly. All plants benefit from regular fertilization, water and correct light levels. Pruning for many varieties is essential for long-term satisfaction. For example, yews perform best when kept pruned. An unpruned, leggy, strung-out look will lead to broken branches and overgrowth. However, pruning yews into balls so that the bottoms of the plants receive no light will cause that part to die out, resulting in the loss of all the lower branches. Usually, neglected deciduous shrubs will not bloom to their potential, resulting in fewer flowers and smaller blossoms. For instance, lilacs and forsythia flower best on new growth from the roots. The mistake is often made to prune out the suckers growing at the base of the plant and to leave the older stems.

With more than 60 varieties, junipers come in all shapes and sizes, from six inches tall to more than 20 feet.

The shrubs look towering and empty except at the top where the flowers are sparse. The best solution is to cut them to the ground all the way, with no stubs left. Within one growing season, the new shoots will reach about two to three feet, fully revitalized.

Fill the gap for that first summer with fast-growing large annuals like giant marigolds or plant a temporary replacement shrub in front of the fledgling growth to be moved to another spot in the landscape during the fall transplanting season. If those alternatives don't suit or pruning to the ground is too drastic, I recommend pruning out a third of the old wood right to the ground each year for three consecutive years; eventually, the shrub will be rejuvenated.

Remember that spring-flowering shrubs set their flower buds the autumn before, so prune right after they flower to avoid eliminating all the buds. Use sharp pruning tools to make clean cuts, and rub the pruning blades with alcohol before moving on to the next shrub to decrease the chance of spreading disease from plant to plant.

If you love spiraea and lilac and are committed to planting them at the front entry, seek out their new dwarf varieties. Dwarf plants typically grow very slowly, as little as half an inch a year, therefore requiring almost no pruning and making them predictable and in scale for a long-lived front foundation plan. Dwarf yews, balsam firs, mugho pines, rhododendrons and hemlocks are a few of the evergreens whose full-sized cousins will overwhelm the landscape. Hybridization has produced many fine flowering shrubs like compact peegee hydrangea, dwarf weigela varieties such as 'Rumba' and 'Minuet', dwarf mountain laurel, and dwarf lilacs like 'Miss Kim'.

There are many varieties of plants within a type, some that grow to two feet, some that grow to ten, so check plant tags carefully for mature sizes when purchasing. For instance, there are junipers that creep along the ground, never reaching more

*Dwarf or compact varieties of shrubs, such as (**left to right**) spruce, hydrangea and lilac, are ideal for the front entry, whereas their full-size relatives can often grow to the point where they are overwhelming and need to be removed or cut back.*

Proper landscaping can make a bland front entrance (see the "before" illustration on page 32) strikingly attractive and inviting. Here, the homeowner has remedied several common front entry ills. A long staircase has been broken into two much more manageable flights, which also permitted the construction of planters. The sweeping sidewalk pulls away from the house, allowing room for a garden, and leads guests away from the mudroom door toward the front door, which is set off with attractive plantings.

than four to six inches in height, like 'Blue Rug' or 'Blue Chip'. Some stay around three to four feet like 'Seagreen'. Others, like 'Wichita Blue', 'Skyrocket' and 'Gray Gleam' are completely upright in habit and can grow to over twenty feet in height. Be wary of the potential spread of a juniper when spacing them in the landscape, as some can grow very large in width. There are over 60 different species of juniper, with many more times that in varieties, that grow in every way, shape and size, so don't be fooled by that cute little plant that might have a huge growth potential.

When shrubs are planted too closely together, they don't perform to their potential, and pruning and bed maintenance is very difficult. Lower and side branches die from lack of light, and fertilizing and mulching the beds is a wrestling match. Again, those cute little plants probably looked great when they were first installed, but with the passage of time, the spacing has become improper. To avoid the problem, choose dwarfs or plants that grow to a width of no more than four or five feet. Then, space the plants accordingly. At first, the bed may look sparse, but within five years and through maturity, the landscaping will thrive. If the spaces are too open for satisfaction initially, use annual flowers to plug the holes temporarily.

AN EXISTING, crowded planting bed should be analyzed to determine which plants have been least affected by the lack of space. Poor specimens exhibit empty lower branches and flat sides. Sometimes, the problem won't be evident until the intruding shrub is removed. Inventory the shrubs that look the best and have the most potential for rejuvenation through correct pruning, increased light and fertilization. Redesign and replant the bed with proper spacing, filling in with new dwarf varieties where old species are no longer appropriate. Your "keeper" list may be short if the crowding has occurred over a long period of time. Sometimes, it is just better to start over with a new plan, new shrubs and a more informed outlook.

Form the new plan with a layered planting: the taller growing shrubs to the rear, medium shrubs in the middle, and a skirt of ground cover shrubs or perennials in the foreground. Perennials and ground covers also interrupt and soften the hard edges of a walkway. Be aware that perennials have documented growth potential, so carefully design their placement with size in mind. Overcrowding happens much faster with perennials, usually in the second growing season, and the cluttered bed will scream for a design adjustment. Luckily, perennials are easy to transplant, whereas shrubs pose more of a dilemma and should be given room to breathe from the beginning.

TREES HAVE THEIR OWN set of problems. Not only must their branches and tops be considered, but their roots can spread to many times their heads. Roots must not be disturbed by construction or have soil piled on them. Dwarf trees like 'Sargent' crab apple and conifers like 'Weeping' Norway spruce that grow slowly make excellent focal points in the entry garden, but full-size trees should be avoided at all costs. It's tragic to have to cut down or hack away at a specimen blue spruce or sugar maple because the branches hang on the roof or press against the windows. Foliage will rot siding if branches hold moisture against it, and painting the house will be difficult and may injure plants. Moving large trees is costly and risky, so think ahead and choose properly sized plants to be able to enjoy them through maturity. The front entry will be most inviting if the plantings are in scale with the house and door.

An attractive front entrance need not be elaborate.
By splaying the ends of a well-constructed walkway and incorporating balanced—
but not symmetrical—plantings of shrubbery whose proportions do not overwhelm
the architecture, this homeowner has made a simple entry striking.

Chapter Two

Ring Around the Foundation

Tactics for camouflage & concealment

I SOMETIMES WONDER if there is a landscape epidemic running rampant in North America. A colleague of mine calls the disease Ring Around the Foundation, or RAF. It manifests itself by completely sheathing house foundations in rings of shrubs, typically crew-cut yews, struggling cedars, and junipers of every size and pointy configuration. The cause of the disorder is a larger than necessary show of foundation wall that homeowners are willing to go to desperate ends to conceal.

For all its prevalence, Ring Around the Foundation is a relatively new affliction. Early American residential landscapes mimicked those in Europe, where foundations were never ringed with shrubs. Granted, the excavators built handsome stone foundation walls instead of resorting to concrete and cinder block, so there wasn't a need to "cozy it up" (in the words of one RAF-afflicted homeowner). In those days, patches of daylilies, herbs, or cutting plants at the front entry or dooryard served as enough adornment.

Large foundation show is occasionally unavoidable, or the result of budget constraints. Where underground rock is near the surface, the only alternative to changing the location of a new house is to blast the rock, which is a huge expense. Another reason for foundation show, especially with older homes, is that all or part of the basement level may be above ground. In one such instance, a friend described her feeling as vertigo when she looked up at her old Victorian home whose basement foundation was exposed to a backyard that sloped drastically away from the house.

The nation's building contractors have contributed to the outbreak of a landscaping ill best described as "Ring Around the Foundation." Its most common manifestation is plenty of ugly foundation showing. Here and there, the desperate homeowner will have tried to hide it with a pointed evergreen that only draws attention to the problem.

BUT SOMETIMES there is simply no excuse for foundation show. With new homes, the contractors' bad habit of skimming the homesite of topsoil during excavation results in the house having a mounded appearance with the grade falling away all around. If you are building a new home, insist that the topsoil be piled and reused to bury the foundation. The cost of hauling and spreading hundreds of cubic yards of topsoil to replace what was removed can be in the tens of thousands of dollars, depending on the size of the yard.

Careful attention paid to the installation of the concrete forms used to make foundations, assuring they are to a depth that will only allow six to eight inches of foundation show when the lawn is established, is the best way to prevent RAF in a new home.

If the contractor is long gone, it's necessary to use creative solutions to alleviate excessive foundation show. Interrupting the lines of the building with green pointy plants every few feet is not well informed landscaping and doesn't do any home justice.

Problem

A Small Amount of Foundation Show

A ONE- OR TWO-FOOT BAND of unattractive gray poured concrete encircling a house is the most common

If there are between one and two feet of foundation showing above ground,
merely planting shrubs in front of it is no remedy. It is far more effective to
build a small retaining wall five or more feet out from the foundation.
After being filled with earth, the area between the wall
and the house can be planted.

manifestation of RAF. Far too many home-owners leap to the easiest and ultimately least successful cure: hiding it behind a row of clipped evergreens planted as closely as possible to the foundation.

Remedy
Build a Low Retaining Wall

IF THERE IS AT LEAST A FOOT of above-ground foundation, merely planting in front of it is no more than a Band-Aid solution. It is far more effective to build a retaining wall five or more feet out from the foundation, fill it with earth to cover the excess concrete and then plant at the new level.

For minor foundation shows, the retaining edge need not be large. Bricks and six-inch timbers are readily available retaining materials that will serve nicely. I've also used granite cobblestones, which are each about the size of a loaf of homemade bread, to retain a small amount of soil.

If the height of the edging doesn't allow the entire foundation to be covered, it is perfectly acceptable to slope the soil away from the foundation to meet the top of the edging. Remember to leave enough room for two inches of bark mulch on top of the soil, and allow for settling.

For minor amounts of foundation show, the retaining wall need not be tall—bricks placed on end will do nicely. If the height of the edging doesn't allow the entire foundation to be covered, it is perfectly acceptable to slope the soil gently away from the foundation to meet the top of the edging.

Problem
Foundation Show in Tight Spaces

IF YOUR YARD IS LARGE, the cure for two or three feet of foundation show can be fairly straightforward: truck in enough soil to bring the grade of the yard up to the top of the foundation, and then gently taper it away from the house. But that takes space. What if you own a small city lot, where the neighbor's garage or house—to say nothing of your property line—restricts the distance additional soil may be spread to blend with the existing grade?

One of the clearest illustrations of this problem I have seen occurred when a new kitchen was built onto an existing home. The new addition was beautiful, but it almost brushed against the branches of a nearby stand of old pines. Because of the sloping lot, at least four to five feet of foundation was unavoidably exposed.

Remedy
Retain & Fill

IN THE YARD with the new kitchen addition, a retaining wall was constructed far enough from the house to make a planting bed between the wall and the foundation but close enough to keep excess soil off the roots of the pine trees. It was an ideal solution, not only for that site, but for most small-space foundation-show problems.

In a small space, it is also wise to build the retaining wall as low as possible and slope the soil in the actual planting bed away from the foundation toward the top of the wall to make up the difference.

If the retaining wall is built at the same height as the top of the foundation, the problem of excess foundation show is only accentuated, because the observer sees the wall as just another foundation, especially when standing some distance away.

In small yards, or in yards where trees grow close to the house, two or three feet of foundation show can be hidden by constructing a retaining wall. In the above illustration, the wall has been built far enough away from the house to allow space for an attractive planting bed.

Problem
Most of the Foundation Is Visible

SOMETIMES THERE IS A COMPLETELY exposed story of concrete on one side of the house. This is most common when the home is built on a sloping lot. In such cases, massive foundation show is understandable. But occasionally I also see houses situated on perfectly flat lots that have so much foundation show that they look to have been constructed on top of pedestals. In either case, the problem is the same: a six-foot-tall—or more—wall of concrete or cinder block to hide.

Remedy
Retain & Back Fill

IF THERE IS LOTS OF SPACE to spread the soil so that it blends with existing grades, no retaining is necessary. However, when the foundation show is significant, even a moderately large lot will require some retaining. In cases where the lot slopes dramatically, a retaining wall will be necessary no matter how much surrounding land you have. When the grade falls away on the entire circumference of the home, filling and retaining will provide the added advantage of a plateau for outdoor living space that is contiguous with porches or living rooms. In the front yard, it allows entering the house at nearly the same level as the door.

You can also turn a steep grade to aesthetic advantage. Filling and retaining allows plenty of opportunity to add ornamental walls and terraces stepping down as many levels as desired. Conversely, if you don't like the sight of walls and terraces, it is entirely possible to fill to the desired level and retain at unseen angles on both sides of the house.

The first step for filling is to figure out how much soil is needed, in cubic yards, by using a transit, a hand-held or tripod-mounted device that determines the difference between the highest and lowest grades.

Depending on how big a space is being filled, a plate compactor, either a hand-pushed model or a large roller on which the operator sits, will have to be called into play. The plate compactor mechanically vibrates soil particles to compact them with weight and motion. Whether you roll or push, it is important to compact each layer of fill, foot by foot, to eliminate sinkholes, which will be a plague forever. Rocks may be used to help fill, but avoid any material that will decompose, leaving depressions behind. For this reason, be sure to grind tree stumps to chips before covering them.

Since filling the entire yard is a large undertaking, it's possible to cheat on the lower levels by using gravel or less expensive soil, free

In some cases, there is nearly a complete story of exposed concrete on one or more sides of a home. Grading will never do the job of concealment, regardless of the lot's size.

The solution to massive amounts of visible foundation is almost always to build a retaining wall. Filling and retaining provides the opportunity to add attractive walls and terraces. Conversely, if you don't like the sight of walls and terraces, you can retain at unseen angles.

of construction debris, as long as it drains well. The top few levels should be soil, and the last six inches should be topsoil suitable for lawn installation. It is prudent to stop filling once the soil is within six inches of the house's siding to prevent rotting or mildew.

If trees are growing in the yard, decide if they are worth saving. Keeper trees will have to be welled with retaining walls whose circumferences are equal to the circumference of the crown of the tree. The earth around the base of the tree must be left at the original level or the tree roots will suffocate. It is usually less expensive to plant a new tree at the new level of

the yard after it is filled than to well around a tree and gamble on survivability.

I've also been in yards where so much soil has been removed from around the trees during excavation that the roots are sticking out of the ground. Cover roots to their original level as soon as possible, although, depending on how long they have been exposed, don't count on survival.

If the retaining wall is to be installed at an unseen angle, choose wall material that is relatively inexpensive. Concrete wall systems and pressure-treated timbers may lack charm and beauty, but they are two good choices to con-

Transits determine the difference between the highest and lowest points of a yard.

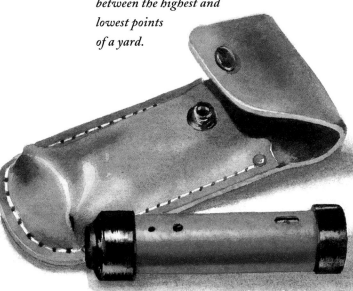

sider if the wall is to be out of sight. Concrete wall systems are perhaps the easiest to install, and seem to have been designed with the homeowner in mind.

ANOTHER RETAINING METHOD that should be considered for both visible and invisible locations is called rip-rap. In rip-rap, large rocks are used, but rather than being stacked on top of one another, as for a wall, they are nestled against each other to cover the surface of an incline.

Leave pockets for perennials and annuals between the stones to soften the harshness of the rock and break up the monotony. Even when retaining a steep area where the stones must be close together, alpine perennials like sedum and hens-and-chicks will fill the gaps and crawl on the rip-rapped rocks.

Trees behind retaining walls either have to be removed or welled. The earth around the base of the tree must be left at its original level or the tree will die.

All of the materials I've mentioned for walls are functional—some are more pleasing to the eye than others—but there is no match for an expertly laid dry-stack stone wall—a work of art. (For a detailed discussion of retaining-wall building techniques, please see Chapter Three.)

Finish off the yard with walkways, patios, decks, plantings and a seeded or sodded lawn. The plantings, layered, spaced properly and presumably raised to the proper height, will be the finishing touch that will truly "ground" your home. Stay with dwarf plants and low growers to retain perspective and minimize maintenance.

Dwarf conifers like Serbian spruce (*Picea*

Filling an entire yard to bring the grade up to the level of the top of the foundation is a huge undertaking. Fortunately, you can "cheat" on lower levels by using gravel. The top few levels should be soil, and the uppermost six inches should be topsoil suitable for seeding with grass. It is important to compact each layer of fill to eliminate sinkholes.

---

omorika 'Nana'), which has a bluish tinge of color, and dwarf balsam fir (*Abies balsama* 'Nana'), a rich, tidy, dark green alternative to the faster-growing yew, are perfect for front foundation plantings. Slow-growth and natural round formations reduce pruning needs and provide long-lived background for colorful dwarf shrubs like 'Emerald Gaiety' euonymus with its variegated white-edged leaves.

For spring flowers, plant dwarf weigela varieties like *Weigela florida* 'Rumba' and 'Minuet', and pink, compact 'Little Princess' spiraea. Herbaceous perennials complete the layered look, but do die back during the cold months.

The visibility of retaining walls, particularly those constructed of less ornamental materials, can be effectively minimized with plants that hang over them. 'Blue Chip' juniper, an improved variety of the old stand-by 'Blue Rug', produces long, blue-colored evergreen runners. An extremely hardy fragrant sumac, *Rhus aromatica* 'Gro-Low' will provide fall color, aromatic leaves and fast coverage for retaining walls.

Whether the job is as small as covering a foot of foundation or as large as filling the entire front or backyard to bring the grade to where it should be, curing Ring Around the Foundation results in an amazing metamorphosis for your yard. You'll find it well worth the effort and expense.

Chapter Three

Ups & Downs

How to turn a hillside to your advantage

I LIVE IN VERMONT, where level ground is at a premium. Our house is built into the side of a mountain, causing my oldest children to climb a half mile uphill from the school bus on a driveway that can be a hardship for four-wheel-drive vehicles. Even once they arrive at the house, their problems are not over. There is a drop of thirty vertical feet between our house and the children's play area.

A neighbor of mine, living with a smaller but equally steep incline, rigged a device to mow the slope leading to the road in front of his house. For years, I've watched him pull his gas-operated lawn mower, tethered with a line of rope, hand over hand, up the slope, then slowly lower it back down by the same method. He's now in his 90s, and I doubt that ritual will continue much longer. His immediate neighbors have left their slopes to the whims of nature, which, depending on the season and the observer's environmental slant, either look wildly native or wretchedly messy.

There are sound safety reasons for my elderly neighbor's approach to mowing his slope. A steep incline can pose real danger if you try to maintain it with power equipment, as my husband, Chris, knows from firsthand experience. He had a scary five days in the hospital after a rototiller he was operating in our front yard started to fall down the slope, and, in his effort to save it, he walked into the rotating tines. All turned out well, but the "killer tiller," as we now call it, hasn't been touched since.

Problem

Dangerous, Unsightly, Inaccessible Slopes

EVEN IF YOU DON'T LIVE on a mountain, slopes are a natural or, sometimes, unnatural part of the landscape. A minor change in grade may be acceptable for most yards, but not if it occurs where the walkway or patio should be. The riser in a step is a "mini" retaining wall that solves a sloping

---

It goes without saying that a steep slope is both potentially dangerous and a maintenance nightmare. Slight slopes, such as the one illustrated here, are not necessarily undesirable. But if they occur where a walkway or patio should go, action must be taken. Sometimes the problem can be solved by building a step or two. If the slope is severe, some sort of retaining wall becomes a necessity.

walkway problem, but when the area is more expansive and the degree of slope greater, a larger solution is necessary.

Remedy

Build a Retaining Wall

ALL SLOPE-RELATED NIGHTMARES, —maintenance, unsightliness, danger and inaccessibility—can be virtually eliminated by the construction of properly designed retaining walls.

When planning retaining walls, try to reduce the massiveness of the project by terracing and planting. Terracing lessens the feeling of being walled in. In a residential yard, waist-to shoulder-high retainers that step incrementally with the grade are in comfortable scale. Creating a series of levels allows for planting spaces as well as patio or deck areas, depending on how far apart the retainers are. Of course, the number of terraces also depends on the height of the slope.

If access to the house involves negotiating a slope, terracing eliminates continuous stair climbing. Landings built on each terrace provide places to rest before mounting the next set of steps. Plantings that hang over the walls or stand in front of them attractively minimize the impact of the walls.

With retaining walls and terraces, the degree of formality created is usually dependent on the shape of the walls and the material out of which they are constructed. Actually, those elements are interrelated. A stately Georgian home dictates the use of formal-looking materials like brick with symmetrical lines, while a country house should use informal, natural flowing curves and materials.

All of the problems associated with the slope on the facing page—
maintenance difficulties, unsightliness and slippery conditions—have been
solved with the addition of an attractive stone retaining wall and two additional
flights of steps. Plantings around the base of the retaining wall
effectively minimize its visual impact.

While there is no hard-and-fast rule about what material and construction techniques should be used for a retaining wall, it is very important to keep in mind that the style of the wall must suit the home. A stately Georgian home like the one above calls for the use of formal-looking material like brick. The straight, symmetrical lines of the home are reflected in the lines of the wall.

Straight walls are fine, but pay careful attention to how they relate to the house. Sometimes it is safer not to try to match the walls of the house with parallel retaining walls. If they aren't exactly right, they will look carelessly built. Angling the retainers avoids that problem and creates an opportunity for interesting design. My own home is built into a mountain. Three sides of the basement are buried, but the front is exposed. We enlarged the usable outdoor space on that side by building a retaining wall at an angle away from the corner. The angle not only makes the wall less obtrusive than if it had come straight out from the house, but gives us more space in the yard. Use props like a garden hose or two-by-four pieces of wood to simulate the lines of the walls, then step back to view the whole picture of house and retainers. Make sure the design is cohesive before starting to excavate and build.

Problem
Walls Built from the Wrong Material

Often, the type of material chosen is a function of what is at hand in the most abundance. In the Caribbean, I saw a unique retainer built entirely of empty, discarded conch shells. Automobile tires horizontally embedded in the ground and stacked one on top of the other are a common sight along the steep shores of Lake Champlain where they double as boat fenders. Whatever their origin, retaining-wall materials must be chosen carefully for long-term strength, building quality, and attractiveness.

In the home below, the wall builder has chosen natural fieldstone, as opposed to the brick used for the wall in front of the house on the facing page. The stone, combined with a wall that curves gently away from the house, creates a natural effect that matches the traditional rural character of the home. Notice that there has been no attempt to duplicate the rigid symmetry of the landscaping in front of the Georgian home in either the retaining walls or the natural-looking plantings.

Remedy 1
Rip-Rap

WHERE STONE IS IN ABUNDANCE, least expensive by far is the retaining method called rip-rap. We're lucky in the Northeast; farmers are constantly plowing up rocks and stockpiling them in abandoned fields. We also have an unlimited supply from area quarries and old walls hidden by overgrowth. Non-native stone from surrounding states is readily available by the pallet or in bulk truckloads.

Ideal rip-rap boulders are rounded and a bit larger than a kettle-style charcoal grill. The one big drawback to rip-rap is that a machine and operator are necessary to move the boulders. Most small skid steer front-end loaders (often called Bobcats, after the loader of that brand name) are only able to lift rocks that weigh less than 1,200 pounds each. But they can squeeze into tight areas and turn on a dime. Also, their large tires are less likely to tear up lawns. Rental dealers have day rates, and the cost can be shared with a neighbor if he has a project too.

Whether you rent the machine yourself or hire an operator and his skid steer, rip-rap installation is a two-person job. One person handles the machine and the other directs by choosing a rock from the pile, then, using hand signals and a crowbar, helps to place it. Rip-rap is not haphazard; it is the careful and deliberate stacking of stone beside stone.

Rip-rap is an affordable, effective retaining wall material. Ideal rip-rap boulders should be the size of a kettle-style charcoal grill, so a machine is necessary for their installation. A proper rip-rap wall will have pockets between some of the boulders for plants.

*Pressure-treated wood is now the least expensive rot-resistant wood available,
and it makes an excellent choice for retaining walls. It comes in six- or eight-inch
widths—convenient for making built-in stairs—and is usually eight or ten feet long.
The "stepping" technique, illustrated to the left of the steps, allows you to move
down a slope more naturally than ending with a squared-off corner.*

Rocks are placed leaning into the slope, beginning from the bottom up, of course. The best rip-rap tries to match the edges of the rocks so that they fit together well. The higher the wall, the closer together the boulders should be, but always leave some space for pockets of soil between them. Perennial plants, especially alpines and succulents like sedum and hens and chicks, love to crawl around the stones, adding a natural, colorful display that breaks up the monotonous web of rock. Rip-rap is one instance where large, high walls are acceptable, because the plantings draw the eye and minimize the imposition of the wall. Stone steps can be built into the rip-rap wall by using huge flat rocks dug into

the slope. Avoid uneven risers by carefully measuring and leveling, because all rocks are not created equal!

Remedy 2
Timber Retainers

WHEN I FIRST STARTED in the landscaping business, used railroad ties were the material of choice for retainers. They were abundant and cheap. However, what they saved in money they made up for in wasted time, ruined clothing and burned flesh. Their inconsistent sizing forced repeated measuring and removal of unusable sections causing a great deal of waste. Creosoted for preservation, the ties ruined clothing and, under a hot sun, produced major burns on the skin. If those reasons aren't enough to avoid them, remember railroad ties are used—well used. They break apart and don't last. I will not use railroad ties today. Thankfully, they have been rendered obsolete.

In the 1970s, the demand for rot-resistant alternatives to rainforest woods and expensive western redwood led to the introduction of pressure-treated wood. At first, pressure-treated wood, too, had problems associated with the safety of preservative chemicals. But now the treatment process has improved. If it is installed using proper precautions, pressure-treated wood is the least expensive type of nonrotting, insect-repelling wood available. When handling pressure-treated wood, wear gloves, protective clothing, goggles and a mask to avoid breathing the dust. The timbers are regular in size (6-inch by 6-inch by 8 to 16 feet, 6-inch by 8-inch by 8 to 16 feet or 8-inch by 8-inch by 8 to 16 feet) and easy to cut and fit. We use a 16-inch circular saw instead of a chainsaw because it leaves clean, smooth edges, and mitered and angled cuts are easily made. (A portable circular saw can be rented for about $25 a day.) Finally, 12-inch-long galvanized common spikes are needed to join the timbers.

Other nonrotting woods available in 6- or 8-inch by 6-inch dimension may be hard to find, of rainforest origin, or very expensive. Those include redwood and cedar and various tropical woods such as greenheart.

Do not try to "cut corners" in the timber wall's infrastructure to save money. I have seen many a timber wall buckled and decrepit because proper construction methods were bypassed. Starting with the second level, at every other tier and at eight-foot intervals, a timber

must be set perpendicular to the face of the wall. The perpendicular members should alternate position from tier to tier to provide strength throughout. Called "deadmen," these timbers should usually be left full length (depending on the ultimate height of the wall) and be included in a crib structure behind the wall. Do not use deadmen in the top layer because they will show on the surface and play havoc with the lawn mower. The unseen construction behind the wall is often more intricate and involved than what is visible, and it is necessary in order to withstand the pressure exerted by tons of roots, water and soil.

To prevent buckling, timbers called "deadmen" must be run back from the wall at least every eight feet and on every other tier. They are connected to a crib structure and buried.

Your wall can move down a slope more naturally if you eliminate or cut short the top timber or timbers until you reach level ground, a method called stepping. Bevel or saw off the square, blunt ends of the timbers to make a smooth-looking finish.

To decrease the impact of a large retainer, terrace the wall, leaving planting or patio space. Steps can be built into the wall or constructed separately and attached in front.

Most manufacturers recommend allowing pressure-treated wood to dry for a year before staining. I dislike the artificial yellow-green color of fresh pressure-treated wood, but once it ages, it blends quite well with nature's colors. Sometimes, staining a structure to blend with the surroundings creates the opposite effect: it sticks out like a sore thumb. I recommend living with the new wall for a year. This allows time to watch it age before making the staining decision. It is wise to wait to plant near the wall until after staining, because the plants risk injury or death from drips and spills. Covering the plants to protect them can cause breakage and/or burning from overheating in the blazing sun.

Uneven and prone to rot, railroad ties are a poor choice for landscaping. And that is only one of the problems with the entrance shown above. The homeowner has attempted to get away without a retaining wall, but the slope is too steep for that shortcut.

Concrete Retaining-Wall Systems

CONCRETE WALLS may be easy to construct, but aesthetically, plain concrete pales next to real stone. Fortunately there is an alternative: the new concrete wall systems that simulate natural stone in color, texture, and shape.

North America was first blessed with massive concrete retaining walls along our major highways years ago. Greatly reduced in scale from commercial applications, the systems available to homeowners are versatile and easy to construct. Although the material is more expensive than natural stone, it is less costly to build with and requires far less skill. There are many systems available, each with its own method of fitting together. Some systems use fiberglass pins between the blocks while others have ridges and channels that fit together. All systems have capstones (the topmost blocks used to complete the wall) to create a smooth, level finish.

I urge caution when choosing a concrete wall system. Some systems simply are not made to be built higher than three to four feet. (The manufacturer may not admit to it.) If in doubt, remember that terracing the walls eliminates this problem completely, while creating another opportunity for patios and planting.

The beauty of some concrete wall systems is that they have blocks especially for straight walls as well as radius blocks to make curved walls. In some systems, stairs can be formed out of blocks that fit directly into the wall.

No matter which system is used, the hardest part of construction is proper installation of the first layer of the wall. Step one should always be to excavate and remove about a foot

*Using a concrete retaining-wall system effectively cures the landscaping ills
of the home on the facing page. Notice how the homeowner has broken the stairs with
a landing. The two terraces are much less imposing than a single wall would have been
and have the added advantage of allowing space for planters. Plants soften the impact
of the bare concrete and add visual appeal to what is now
a functional, attractive entrance.*

of material beneath what will eventually become the base of the wall, unless the soil is well drained and gravelly. Dig a hole a little wider and longer than the final wall size. Next, backfill it with gravel free of construction debris. Then, tamp with a hand tamper or gas-powered plate compactor until the surface is well compressed. Finally, begin the first layer, using a construction level to place each block. Lay out the entire first level of blocks before starting the second. When the first layer is leveled,

just keep stacking the blocks according to the manufacturer's suggestion, up to the height of choice.

Finishing any wall requires a final level of block known as capstones. There are many options at the cap level. Most systems provide concrete capstones that fit into the block below but have a flat, even surface on top. A dressier option is to match another material already used in the landscape design like bluestone in the walkway nearby. To maintain continuity and keep the plan from being busy, avoid introducing an entirely new substance.

Bluestone or other flat stone should be cantilevered about an inch over the concrete block to make an attractive finish. If I've designed a curved wall, the bluestone cap is cut to follow the curve as well. A masonry bonding agent available in tubes like caulk must be inserted between the cap and the top block. That way, if someone sits on the wall or bumps against it, the capstone will stay in place. Other natural stone caps like slate, granite, marble or flat fieldstone should be bonded to the top level of blocks as well.

Remedy 4
Dry-Stack Stone Walls

THERE ARE TOWNS in New England where stone fences have delineated properties and pastures for decades—even centuries. The artisans who built those walls knew how to lay the stone so that it would withstand the test of time.

Unfortunately, most of those artisans died without passing on their craft to the next generation, probably because the walls were born out of need and abundance of material rather than choice and aesthetics. With the advent of barbed-wire fencing, laying stone became menial hand labor. To a degree, the same holds true today. Where rocks are found in abundance, building a wall of natural stone results in great savings in material costs. However, any savings can quickly be eaten up by labor. Properly constructed stonework is slow and deliberate.

Be very careful when choosing rocks for wall building. Some stone can shatter with freeze/thaw fluctuations and therefore is totally unsuitable. Stay away from rock that plates or separates easily. One way to avoid bad stone is to ask the supplier for site examples that have been in place for at least two years. Look for telltale signs of deterioration like cracks, fallen shards and collapsing walls.

Base preparation for natural rock walls is the same as for concrete wall systems: a foot of excavation, wider and longer than the finished wall, gravel backfill, and mechanical or hand compaction with a tamper. The difference is that with natural stone, the bottom of the wall must be wider than the top. For instance, a completed three-foot-high wall will be three feet wide at the bottom and can taper to two feet at the top. Stagger the joints of the wall from course to course for stability.

The key to a beautiful wall is how well the builder "works the stone," an expression whose meaning becomes clear in the thick of construction. Hand chisels and hammers are necessary as well as a keen eye for shapes. Each stone, no matter whether flat like slate or other quarried stone or rounded like fieldstone, should fit with its neighbors in perfect union.

When a truckload of stone is delivered and dumped, it is often hard to see the forest for the trees. Some landscapers affec-

*Although properly constructed stone retaining walls can be expensive
and inevitably take a great amount of time to build, nothing matches them for pure
aesthetic appeal in the right setting. Built well, they can last for decades—even centuries.
The key is to choose stone that will not shatter in freeze/thaw cycles. "Working the stone"
requires hammers and hand chisels as well as a keen eye for shape. Joints must
always be staggered, and each stone must fit snugly with its neighbors.
Square corners, **left**, give the wall a finished, professional look.*

*Begin constructing a natural stone wall in the same way as you would
a concrete wall. First, excavate a foot-deep trench below the site of the wall.
It should be filled with gravel, which is then compacted. The base of a stone wall is always
wider than the top, so allow for this when excavating. Each stone must be selected individually.
The best way to do this is to spread the stones out over a large area. Capstones on top
of the wall must be exceptionally large and flat, so as building progresses,
set aside likely candidates for later use.*

tionately call it "rock block," the endless wandering among the stones looking for the perfect fit.

One way to reduce "rock block" is to set aside a large area near the building site to spread out the stone. We like palletized stone because we can order a large quantity at one time and spread it out as needed. There will be a huge clean-up job when finished unless a large tarpaulin is laid out under the stone, be-

The last step in stone wall construction is introducing backfill. Before a wall is backfilled,
it is prudent to line the back with erosion cloth that lets water through but keeps out silt and soil.
Clean, one-inch-diameter stone should be placed against the cloth. If these procedures are followed,
the wall will weep properly, and last for generations. If soil and silt clog the spaces between rocks,
water will build up behind the wall, eventually undermining its integrity.

cause there are always pieces that crumble during transportation and handling. Tarpaulin or no tarpaulin, expect to repair the lawn area beneath. The length of time the stone or tarp will be on the ground in the work area will surely ruin or burn the grass under it.

CAPSTONES MUST BE LARGE AND LEVEL. They must also fit together perfectly. When ordering from the supplier, specify capstones so that the load will contain them. As building progresses, set aside likely candidates for later cap use. They should be thick, flat on top, and large enough to stay in place. I have seen walls that are finished without caps, but I don't consider them "finished." If the wall can't be sat on comfortably, it isn't complete.

The last step in wall construction is introducing the backfill. Before a wall is backfilled, it is prudent to line the back of the wall with a spun erosion cloth that lets water permeate but holds silt from seeping through. The cloth, which is sometimes marketed under the name DeWitt Weed Barrier, is available from hardware and home and garden centers in four-foot-wide rolls, which are adequate for low walls and leave some slack to accommodate backfill material. Overlap the cloth for higher walls.

Clean, one-inch-diameter stone that is free of debris should be placed immediately against the cloth to allow proper drainage. Dump in about a foot of the stone next to the cloth, stopping within six inches of the top of the wall to leave room for topsoil. Finally, holding the cloth so it doesn't slip with impact, backfill with soil, then tuck in the cloth so it doesn't show.

Dry stack walls, built properly, withstand the elements because of the continuous weep holes inherent in their structure. If silt and soil are allowed to plug the holes, water will build up, undermining the integrity of the wall.

Even when there's no slope to retain, walls can still be valuable allies to the home landscaper, particularly in parts of the yard where plants refuse to grow. Small-scale retaining walls can raise the soil level above wet areas, hide wellheads and septic pump-outs and provide elevated areas for privacy plantings. It's generally best to keep the walls as low as possible, particularly in northern areas, where freezing can destroy delicate plant roots.

Problem

A Tough-to-Plant Area

EVERY YARD SEEMS to have one of these—an area that cries out for a planting of some sort, but where plants refuse to grow. There can be many reasons: a slightly moist area; an island of grass in the center of a circular driveway that would look much better if it were planted in something more imaginative, but isn't big enough for a mature, spreading shade tree; a large rock or other feature that cannot be removed.

Remedy

Use a Retaining Wall to Make a Planter

MOST OF THE TIME, we think of retaining walls as useful in holding back a slope. But small-scale retaining walls can also be the solution to the problems of hard-to-plant areas if they are used to make small planters.

Concrete wall systems, dry-stack stone walls, or pressure-treated wood walls all work well for that purpose. Timber planters can be constructed a few different ways. Burying timbers on end and securing them with wire underground allows the builder to make a wooden oval or round retainer. A square or rectangular planter can be constructed of horizontally joined timbers, cribbed with deadmen.

Several problems can be solved by building a raised planter. Sometimes the soil is too wet to plant directly, and lifting trees and shrubs above the soaked earth will allow enjoyment of an area of the yard that was unusable. On a small lot where large trees would be overwhelming, a raised planter filled with dense shrubs like red twig dogwood, purple-leaf sand cherry, and full-sized lilacs, especially late lilacs such as 'James McFarlane' and small trees like amur maple will provide privacy screening. Finally, when trying to hide a conspicuous wellhead, septic-clean out, or similar unattractive feature, a raised planter will camouflage the problem and still provide access.

I TRY TO KEEP THE RETAINING WALLS of a planter as low as possible, using the plants within to provide the height; otherwise the walls become the focal point. Another justification for shallow planters, especially in northern climates, is the destruction of tender plant roots in subfreezing temperatures if the roots aren't insulated by surrounding soil and a good snow cover. Roots must not be elevated too high, because they will be exposed to the elements. In a raised space, plants with large root systems should be placed towards the middle, while small shrubs and herbaceous perennials can form the border. Keep all plants at least eighteen inches from the retaining wall to guard against contact that will cause the roots to dry out or freeze. I have been unsuccessful with lining planters with foam insulating board or covering plants within to protect them from the elements. When I just can't keep the edge plants, I use annuals.

Problem
Too Much Wall Showing

THERE IS NO DOUBT that retaining walls are functional. They can even be aesthetically pleasing. But unless your wall is hand fashioned from beautiful fieldstone, its easy to get too much of a good thing. Let's face it: long unbroken lengths of retaining wall are not attractive.

Remedy
Break It Up With Plants

THE BEST WAY to minimize the impact of retaining walls is to use plants that hang over the walls. 'Blue Rug' or 'Blue Chip' junipers, fragrant sumac, euonymus 'Emerald Gaiety' or 'Emerald and Gold', and *Cotoneaster praecox* all creep along the ground until they reach the wall and spill over to hang in front. Vines like English ivy will crawl as ground covers before they reach the edge and slip over.

Planting on the ground in front of the wall also softens its imposition. Choose plants that, at maturity, will reach within a foot or two of the top of the wall so that they will be in scale with the wall. I prefer to cluster a planting and leave some wall exposed rather than line up the plants along the wall like little soldiers. Instead of minimizing the lines of the wall, a row of plants will emphasize its length and breadth. Layer the clustered planting with the taller shrubs to the rear, shorter shrubs in the middle and a skirt of perennials or ground cover at the front edge. The focal point will be the planting, not the wall.

Chapter Four

Good Fences

Attractive barriers for safety & privacy

WHEN WE TOOK POSSESSION of our lakeside cottage a few summers ago, my raucous family of five shattered the serenity the elderly couple next door had enjoyed for the past thirty-two years. Matters were made worse when we adopted a ninety-pound mutt named Sam, who just loves to "talk" to every person, boat and dog that cruises past our tiny piece of land. Hemmed in by property-line constraints, we planned a fence to test the adage "good fences make good neighbors."

Of course, you don't need to live on the lakefront to warrant having a fence. Fencing serves many purposes, as evidenced by an acquaintance of mine who lives on a busy street corner and was bothered by automobile headlights striking her windows every evening. Suburbanites and city dwellers lack the luxury of acres of buffering property and trees and may want to screen out the neighbors or screen in family activity. Families with roving dogs and small children may want the security of a fenced yard or play area.

Some confined areas such as pools and dog runs may at first dictate the use of a chain-link fence. But although it is functional, chain link is unattractive. Fortunately, more creative materials can serve the same purpose. Here, a rural swimming pool is surrounded by a post-and-split-rail fence that has been lined with wire-mesh fencing, which provides support for vines.

Problem

A Lack of Privacy or A Need for Safety

THERE'S NO DOUBT THAT FENCES have their uses. When you find yourself suffering from the fish bowl effect of a condominium or an urban lot, a stockade fence is a sure way to create privacy. The same fence will also buffer street noises. Chain-link fences can confine prone-to-wander animals. And they can provide safe play areas for youngsters. In some municipalities, a fence is required by law around pools.

The catch for the homeowner is how to enjoy the practical advantages of a fence without having to live with an eyesore.

Remedy

Build an Attractive Fence

MOST EVERYONE IS FAMILIAR with fencing's two standbys: chain-link fencing and wooden stockade enclosures. But there are also several affordable and more attractive alternatives to those styles sold through home and garden centers, and there is always the limitless imagination and creativity of a handy do-it-yourselfer's custom design. As with most landscaping remedies, it's important to match the design of the fence to the function it's expected to serve.

Some reasons for fencing may require unconventional plans, like my friend's on the busy village corner. The fence she eventually built created privacy as well as a shield from beaming headlights. At her location, a multi-level picket-style fence avoided making a walled-in feeling by being built only to waist level where screening was not needed. The resulting courtyard is so tranquil that it is now a haven for hungry birds. The traditional white picket style also blended well with my friend's home, a nineteenth century New England cottage, and it mimicked the fencing across the street. I always try to match fencing with architectural features, indigenous materials and regional flavor so the fence belongs to and enhances the landscape instead of dominating it: painted white picket in New England or rural Virginia, redwood contemporary in California, brick and wrought iron in New York City or Boston, adobe in the southwest.

Some confined areas—dog runs and pools, for example—may at first seem to dictate the use of chain-link fencing. However functionally appropriate it may be, chain link is never much to look at. Fortunately, more creative materials can serve the same purpose. I've used a post-and-split-rail fence to enclose a rural

---

Another alternative to chain-link fencing, aluminum fencing goes well in a formal setting. Dressy in appearance, black aluminum fencing almost disappears if placed in front of landscape features like trees. The spindles of the fence are spaced close enough together to keep little bodies out and slim enough to be unimposing. Aluminum fencing is usually manufactured in six-foot sections and comes in different heights and spindle designs.

Augment existing stockade fencing with lattice, which enhances the fence and provides a ladder for climbing vines and espaliered trees and shrubs, such as the dwarf crab apple illustrated above.

swimming pool, and lined the fence with green vinyl-coated hardware cloth tacked to the posts on the inside. The hardware cloth provided support for vigorous vines like honeysuckle and climbing roses, while it prevented children and animals from entering the pool area. The informal style wasn't distracting and enhanced the view from house to pool patio and the surrounding countryside.

Formal and dressy in appearance and perception, black aluminum fencing almost disappears in the landscape. The spindles of the fencing are spaced close enough together to keep little bodies out, yet slim enough to be unimposing. Aluminum fencing usually is manufactured in six foot sections and is available in different heights and spindle designs.

I never thought I would be an advocate of plastic anything, let alone fencing, but from a maintenance standpoint, PVC fencing is ideal. In some cases, I have actually had to touch the fencing to realize it wasn't wood. It never needs painting, and a good hosing restores it to like-new condition. Originally developed for horse confinement because horses won't chew PVC, the post-and-rail-style is appropriate in both country and city settings. Combining post-and-rail PVC fencing with stone pillars built at regular intervals blended beautifully at a stone-faced rural home I landscaped. Don't be afraid to add creative touches to a fence to echo house details, because those touches help blend and unify the design.

WHATEVER MATERIAL you finally choose, fencing can be an expensive proposition. If you purchase a home that has fencing you don't like, consider altering or revamping it to improve its appearance. Sometimes a simple paint or staining job may be enough to improve the fencing. Adding or removing finials (decorative post toppers) from the fence posts may upgrade its appearance and create a more agreeable style.

At a condominium unit or cramped city lot where privacy is at a premium, wooden stockade fencing is often the only way to separate one unit from another. Condo associations usually will not allow residents to eliminate existing features in the landscape, but try augmenting the fencing by attaching lattice. The lattice elegantly enhances an unsightly necessity while providing an avenue for climbing vines and espaliered (a traditional pruning and training technique that requires a vertical surface to wire the plant to) trees and shrubs. Dwarf crab apples and fruit trees lend themselves well to espalier and they bear fruit at a manageable, easy-to-pick height. Other plants often used for espalier are pyracantha, junipers and grapes. Lattice alone can be used for privacy fencing when vines are grown on it.

Another fencing option I've seen and used allows customization by mixing and matching different style panels of wooden fences to create a whole new look. For instance, four-foot-high board-and-batten may be topped by two

---

At a condominium, townhouse or cramped urban lot, where privacy is at a premium, stockade fencing is often the only way to assure privacy. To break up the monotony of the fence, consider customizing it by mixing and matching different styles of preconstructed panels.

The jury is out on what to do with fencing on a slope, but always straighten the posts so they are plumb regardless of variations in grade. In the fence above, the builder has opted for a method called "stepping."

feet of framed trellis to create a six-foot-high privacy fence that is opaque on the bottom but light and airy on the top. Many selections and height variations are available at lumber yards, home centers and garden shops, including gates that can be customized to match the panels.

REGARDLESS OF ITS STYLE, all fencing requires the digging of post holes. The depth of the holes will vary depending on the style of fence, the length of the posts, and the freeze-thaw extremes of the local climate. In the Northeast and colder parts of the country, deep frost can heave posts out of the soil. Burying six inches of post for every foot exposed above the ground will be adequate for most areas. In other words, a four-foot post above the ground will have two feet buried.

While digging postholes may be a commonplace activity for farmers, most homeowners install fencing once or twice in a lifetime. For that reason, renting rather than owning the mechanical tools of the trade is probably a wise decision. Hand-held manual posthole diggers will do the job if soil is light and free of rocks and are especially helpful in cleaning up the hole a mechanical auger makes. When installing slim fence posts like the aluminum ones, rent a two-person auger to make the digging easier, while for thick posts, use a tractor-mounted PTO (power take-off) auger.

A two-person auger has opposite handles mounted at the top with a screw-shaped bit on the bottom. The gas-powered motor is located at the top, and the handles are used to brace the machine while it is digging. A tractor-mounted auger with a large bit is recom-

For a more natural look than the one opposite, do not step the fence; allow it to follow the grade. To make sure corners are square, measure 3 feet down one leg, 4 feet down the other, and ensure that the hypotenuse (diagonal) is 5 feet. (Or use multiples of these ratios, such as 6, 8 and 10 feet.)

---

mended for thick posts, because if a large bit is attached to a two-man auger, it can send the operators into orbit when it hits a rock.

No matter what implement is chosen, it is very important to note that digging all the holes ahead of time may not be a time saver. Often there are calculation adjustments along the way due to fence post inconsistencies and the presence of rocks. If the calculations are off, two inches can quickly become six inches, six inches a foot, and the holes will have to be dug again.

T HE JURY IS OUT on what to do on a slope with fencing, but always straighten the posts so they are plumb regardless of the grade variations. The fencing can be stepped along the slope, or

if the fencing is composed of prefabricated panels, some styles can actually be twisted at their fastening axes, resulting in a parallelogram shape that follows the grade.

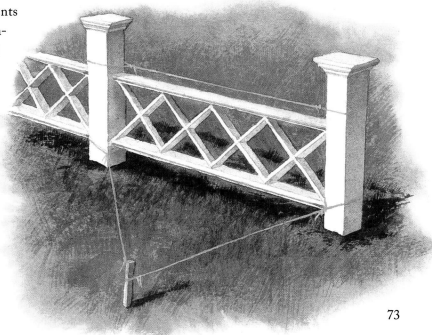

If custom building the fencing on site or using post and rail fencing, decide whether to follow the slope or step the fence sections. My preference is to follow the slope because it is more natural and therefore less conspicuous.

We partially backfill holes for aluminum fence posts with concrete for stability. Wooden posts that cannot be buried to the proper depth because they hit an obstruction are given the same treatment. Whether you use concrete or just the soil you dug out, backfilling of the holes should be thorough and

---

Finishing touches and details can make the whole difference in distinguishing a fence style. Prefabricated finials (post toppers) can be purchased at home-building stores. But you can also custom fashion finials, post heads and pickets.

compacted, with no air pockets left to cause instability or capture water that will heave the posts in freeze-thaw fluctuations. A hand tamper (a long-handled, flat-headed tool) will compact the soil properly. In heavy soils, use processed gravel backfill. It will prevent having to break up clumps of clay. The gravel packs well and sets up like concrete.

Sometimes, finishing touches or details can make the whole difference in distinguishing a fence style. Prefabricated finials (post toppers) can be purchased in a home building store. Of course, by using imagination and carpentry skills, you can custom fashion finials, post heads or pickets by creating a paper template for the top of the pickets and cutting them out with a jigsaw.

Problem

Plenty of Space, But a Lack of Privacy

IT IS NOT ONLY URBANITES and owners of small lots who feel the effects of a lack of privacy. Ironically, if the lot is expansive, a simple fence might not do an effective job of screening unsightly buildings or blunting noise.

Remedy

Grow a Living Fence

MANY PEOPLE CHOOSE TREES for screening and privacy. Trees also buffer wind, muffle noise and provide shade to cool the home and outdoor living areas. Consider the size of your property, the soil conditions and the purpose of the plant

In a living fence, it is a good idea, whenever possible, to use several different types of plants rather than practicing monoculture. An informal, mixed screen of deciduous and evergreen trees and shrubs allows diversity of color and texture and creates the opportunity for four-season appeal. Informal plantings can include pines, firs, viburnums and lilacs. If the hedge is to serve as a windbreak, however, avoid white pines and hemlocks. They can be burned by the wind.

buffer in order to choose the appropriate species of trees or shrubs. Usually, a great deal more space is needed for a living fence than for its structural counterpart.

Don't make the mistake of bringing home those cute little potted seedlings and expecting them to stay little. Learn about their growth potential and remember that plants not only grow up, they grow out. Whatever extends onto the neighbor's property is his to prune and maintain, which isn't always good news to the neighbor or to the plant. I have seen many a hack job due to an improper plant choice. Locating a privacy hedge on the property line is inviting trouble, because the neighbor is free to prune his or her side of the hedge if it grows to the point where it is "trespassing."

If the purpose of the plant buffer is for privacy, choose a dense evergreen such as red or Austrian pine or Douglas or balsam fir for year-round screening. If the yard is small, pick an upright grower like arborvitae or juniper. Make sure the plant choice is a species that will keep its lower branches into maturity whether it grows wide or stays narrow. Although most any evergreen will lose branches as the upper ones shade the lower ones, the spruce family is especially prone, so don't choose blue or Norway spruce for screening. Never plant under utility lines unless the chosen plant will stay small into maturity. Also, beware of roadway and utility rights-of-way. Sides of public roads usually belong to the highway departments and utilities, although they often appear to be part of the yard. It is most discouraging to witness the removal of a mature screen planting when roads are widened or telephone poles moved.

SPACE LIMITATIONS and personal taste will decide whether it is prudent to plant a hedge in a straight row or to plant it in an informal, natural way, alternating the plants and mixing species. Whenever possible, it is a good idea to use several different types of plants rather than to practice monoculture. If a disease or insect infests a species, it will be confined to that plant rather than possibly destroying the entire hedge. An informal, mixed screen of deciduous and evergreen trees and shrubs allows diversity of color and texture and creates the opportunity for four-season appeal featuring flowers, berries and autumn color.

Typical plants used for a formal, single-file hedge include arborvitae, hemlock, spiraea, 'Tallhedge' buckthorn, barberry and privet because they all adapt well to pruning and being kept small. Informal plantings are often made up of larger species and may include pines and firs, viburnums, lilacs and heavy shade trees like maples, ash, and oak. If the informal arrangement is primarily intended to serve as a windbreak, choose plants for their ability to withstand drying winter sun and wind, avoiding white pine and hemlock because they burn easily.

A living fence is an appropriate alternative to other fencing, but only an unlimited budget will provide instant screening, as large trees are expensive and difficult to handle and plant. Using foresight, it is smart to plant quick, inexpensive, short-lived growers like Russian olive (grows wide) and Lombardy poplar (upright) as interim screening, mixed with long lived, small, affordable trees and shrubs that take their time to fill the space.

In a few years, when the Russian olives have become leggy, spindly, and broken—and they will, because it's inherent in their nature—the better species will have matured enough to solve the screening problem.

If the purpose of the living fence is to provide privacy, choose a dense evergreen. Austrian pines or Douglas firs do well if there is a great deal of room, but in smaller areas, pick upright growers like arborvitae or juniper, **above.** *Members of the spruce family, particularly blue and Norway spruce, should be avoided because they lose their lower branches over time.*

Chapter Five

Out of Sight, Out of Mind

How to hide an unattractive feature

I HAVE OFTEN WONDERED what it is about excavators, contractors and utility company employees that causes them to place obtrusive features such as wellheads, septic mounds, propane tanks, electric meters, hatch doors leading to basements and (my personal pet peeve) big, blocky electric junction boxes in exactly the wrong place—at least from a landscaper's perspective.

Give an electric company installer wide open acres and he or she will inevitably put the junction box directly in the line of sight from the living room windows. With an entire yard to choose from, why does it seem like septic clean-outs are so frequently placed in the only spot where a walkway should go?

Sometimes, I am at a total loss to explain the placement of electric meters. Friends of ours once owned a lovely Victorian stone home. An ugly electric meter had been affixed directly to the hand-cut limestone at eye level only a few feet from the front entrance. Like most meters, theirs had been placed with ease of reading as the only consideration.

The list goes on and on. Everyone has seen examples of what I call the "there's an elephant buried in my yard" syndrome, those squared-off, unnatural-looking septic leach-field mounds that are, as often as not, placed ten feet away from the house.

If you are building a new home, by all means intercept the

Evergreens effectively camouflage these propane tanks, while a stepping-stone path gives full access to anyone coming to service the tanks. It is always important to allow a few feet of room between tanks and shrubs, and when planting the shrubs, keep in mind their eventual size.

subcontractors in time to steer such objects to where they will be least noticed. That way, you'll be able to spend landscaping dollars on installing and planting features that will give pleasure rather than on hiding features that don't.

Unfortunately, most homeowners are not so lucky.

Problem:

Obtrusive Tanks & Meters

TANKS AND METERS MUST be installed with convenience as the primary consideration. But too often convenience

means that the object becomes an ugly blot on the home landscape.

Remedy

Appropriate Plantings and Pathways

THE GREATEST CHALLENGE in disguising unsightly features is making them inconspicuous without looking like you are doing so. As long as the meter or gas tank fill-up is accessible, it's possible to remove it as a focal point by concealing it behind shrubs and trees. However, it is important to make it easy for the meter reader or gas filler to do his or her job; otherwise, inadvertent breakage or destruction of plants or barriers may occur. In fact, encourage the utility person to use a specific path by deliberately providing one.

I once hid propane tanks with hemlocks on a shady corner of a home and installed a stepping-stone path to the tanks that gave full access to the propane filler. The shrubs were spaced three to four feet away from the tanks to allow for growth and maintenance and to avoid harm from spillage. Also, the hemlocks I used were naturally arranged with deciduous clethra—shade-loving, sweet-smelling, midsummer bloomers that softened the corner of the house rather than making it obvious that I was hiding something.

Problem
Wellheads & Electric Junction Boxes.

IT'S BAD ENOUGH that wellheads and electric junction boxes are inevitably placed where they are most visible. And trying to camouflage them with a shrub or two often has an opposite effect than the one desired: it only draws attention to the fact that there is something to hide. The challenge is to make wellheads and junction boxes inconspicuous without it looking like that is what you are trying to do.

Hiding a junction box with plantings works well and, if done properly, need not look contrived. Plants should be chosen for their ability to screen, but their ultimate size should be just large enough to obscure the object.

Remedy
Create a Planting Bed

I T I S IMPORTANT TO ENJOY landscaping from inside the home as well as outside, so it is perfectly acceptable, if not preferable, to have island planting beds in the yard that are easily viewed from the windows. For that reason, hiding a wellhead or junction box with a large planting bed works well and, if done properly, doesn't have to appear contrived.

Always keep in mind, though, that access to the unit may someday be needed. Plants should be chosen for their ability to screen, but their ultimate size should be just large enough to obscure the object. I prefer layered plantings where shrubs of different height are coupled with ground-cover-like shrubs and perennials placed in the foreground. One such island I planted with dwarf peegee hydrangeas, which became so full it was hard to discern one plant from another. The hydrangeas surrounded a cement pumping station for a septic system that sat eighteen inches above the ground and was two and a half feet in diameter. In front of the hydrangeas, low-growing sargent junipers provided an evergreen skirt that served as a buffer or layer between the hydrangeas and the lawn and screened the pumping station when the leaves fell.

Deciduous shrubs provide better accessibility for maintenance, because a pipe or hose can be pushed between the branches. It is still important to allow space, though, so breakage will not occur. Red twig dogwoods, another excellent choice, are natural-looking plants and have outstanding red twig color all winter. The dogwoods are so densely stemmed that a wellhead in the center of an arrangement is invisible summer or winter. Red twig dogwoods are upright growers, so perennials like daylilies, with foliage that spills and falls away from the base of the shrubs, makes a neat border of color in the transition from shrub to lawn.

For me, hiding electric junction boxes poses the greatest challenge. They are never where you want them, and it is impossible to hide them quickly except with an unlimited budget. But over time, plants will grow wide enough to obscure the box—as long as you plant them in a natural design, rather than just circling the box with a few evergreens.

Since these boxes are generally placed at the edge of the property, in rural areas, try to use native or indigenous plants, deciduous and evergreen, in a layered planting that blends with the surrounding vegetation. In a city development, where all the native plants have been stripped away, the boxes can become extremely obvious. Create a screen by mixing evergreen and deciduous species. Arborvitae,

and blue hollies such as *Ilex meserveae* 'Blue Boy' or 'Blue Girl' as well as the old-fashioned Christmas hollies and rambling *Rosa rugosa* shrubs are all good choices for screening. Whatever you choose, be sure to leave the access panel clear.

Hybridizers have developed many "miniature" versions of classic plants that are ideal for low-maintenance plantings around junction boxes. Deciduous examples include dwarf burning bush with bright red autumn color, dwarf peegee hydrangea with its snowball-like flowers, *Viburnum trilobum* 'Compactum' commonly known as American cranberry bush, for its huge clusters of edible red berries, and dwarf varieties of honeysuckle, lilac and spiraea. 'Miss Kim' lilac has profuse, fragrant

red twig dogwood, barberry with red fall color and berries, and wide-spreading junipers mix well for informal naturalizing. Wind-tolerant pines like Austrian and red, viburnums with white flowers and outstanding fall color, hardy holly varieties like *Ilex verticillata* 'Sparkleberry'

A septic pump-out station, **top,** *is masked by dwarf peegee hydrangea with ground-hugging 'Sargent' junipers placed in front to provide an evergreen skirt that both serves as a buffer between the hydrangeas and the lawn, and screens the station year-round.*

purple flowers on a wide-spreading compact shrub, and 'Little Princess' spiraea stays two to three feet tall.

There are many species of pine, fir and spruce that have been developed as dwarfs also, but they grow very slowly. For quick results, it's best to choose evergreens that like to be pruned, such as arborvitae and hemlock. Pay attention to growth rate when choosing plants in the garden center as well as to texture, color and blooming time to create that four-season appeal so important to a successful landscape.

When planting around junction boxes, be careful to watch for wires and pipes. There is a national company known as Dig Safe that will alert your local utility companies to send representatives to your home to locate the underground systems and mark them with orange paint. Dig Safe also has information on the regulations to observe concerning how far away from buried wires it is safe to dig. This service is at no cost. However, failure to contact the company may result in costly repairs or even personal injury. Keep in mind that wires for cable TV, invisible dog fences and low-voltage lighting are not buried very deeply.

Problem
Septic Mounds

IN MOST AREAS, local environmental laws are stringent when it comes to the size, location and make-up of septic leaching fields. To my knowledge, however, no one has written a law that decrees septic mounds must be built in such a way that the unfortunate homeowner is constantly reminded of their presence. Still, in rural areas they remain a necessity. Fortunately, there are ways to lessen their impact through imaginative landscaping.

Remedy
Retaining Walls & Imaginative Grading

AT MY OFFICE, we successfully hid all the components of a septic system—pump station, clean-out and leach field—by enclosing them with a wall and then filling the enclosure with soil up to the level of the septic system's cement protrusions. Since we needed to leave the covers of the pumping station and septic clean-out accessible, I planted around the pipes with fragrant sumac, a native shrub that spread its branches over all the concrete areas. The rest of the enclosure was planted with grass, making the leach field completely invisible. It now looks like a natural slope was retained, and visitors are amazed when told what lies underneath the landscaping.

A house in my neighborhood, which appears in the photograph at the front of this chapter, has a good example of a thoughtfully located septic mound placed well away from the dwelling on a natural-looking angle. The excavator filled the potentially sharp walls of the mound so that a gradual and gentle slope was formed. The surrounding rolling terrain reinforces the shape of the artificial mound. The raised areas provide a buffer from the road and are tucked among several trees that, because of their age, are in scale with the massiveness of the mound.

As refreshing as it is to see a creative solution to the "buried elephant" problem, unless there is excess fill on the property, it may be expensive to truck in the amount needed to disguise the mound. It is also necessary to have the luxury of enough space to make it look like a natural hill. Those who don't have the space or adequate fill will have to look to the retain-

Cellar doors may be convenient, but they can also be unattractive.
A picket fence in keeping with the siding material of the home conceals the cellar
doors, **above,** *but at the same time allows ease of access.*

ing-wall solution I employed at my office.

Another mistake I've often seen is the placement of a septic tank in the direct path of a proposed walkway. In northern climates, it is necessary to excavate at least a foot of original soil beneath a walkway and fill with drainage gravel, but excavation is not recommended over a septic tank. And there's always the challenge of allowing access to the tank for pumping out and other maintenance.

One solution I developed was to design a serpentine walkway of small interlocking concrete pavers looping around the tank. This allowed space for a planting bed between the walk and the house. The septic clean-out is safely buried in the bed, under about three inches of mulch and obscured by plant branches.

Problem

Hiding Hatch-Type Cellar Doors

ANYONE WHO HAS HAD TO LUG armloads of firewood through the house and down a narrow set of steps to a cellar storage area can understand why those hatch-type cellar doors were invented. Opened wide, they provide easy and direct access to the area under a house. But the very traits that make them so convenient also make them intrusive and unattractive. The challenge facing the landscaper is to mask the hatches while still assuring ease of access.

*Although pool machinery can be hidden successfully behind shrubs, provided
that enough elbow room is left for chores, a better solution is to construct tightly latticed fence
around the equipment. Cover the lattice with something like climbing roses and paint
it the same color as the house to make it less obtrusive.*

Consider a Fence or a Latticed Screen

ONE OF THE MOST BLATANT INSTANCES of this problem I've seen was a bulkhead with metal hatches placed within eight feet of a front door. The challenge was to remove the bulkhead and hatches as a focal point. The front yard was filled to cover foundation walls, which allowed us to build a low retaining wall around the doors to partially hide them. A short picket fence was installed to mask the view from the driveway, and a tightly latticed screen was constructed as a support for vines to obscure the view from the entry deck. Now, honeysuckle vines, bird's-nest spruce, and many varieties of perennials capture the eye instead of the metal doors.

Masking the Presence of Pool Machinery

WHEN PEOPLE INSTALL a backyard pool, it seems they almost always spend vast amounts of effort and money landscaping the deck and surrounding yard. This makes sense because during fine summer weather, the pool becomes a focal point for relaxing and entertaining. Unfortunately, the effect of many poolside landscaping projects is ruined by the presence of awkwardly hidden pumps and filters.

Try a Lattice Fence

AS LONG AS PLENTY OF SPACE is left for maintenance (don't hesitate to act out the flushing and filter-cleaning scenario to decide how much space is needed), building a pool house or surrounding pool equipment with shrubs will successfully take care of the problem.

Another, often better, solution is to construct very tightly latticed open-roofed fencing around pool equipment. This allows for air circulation and free access to the machinery while hiding the equipment. Cover the lattice with something like climbing roses and paint it the same color as surrounding structures to make it less obtrusive.

Remember, any time plants are used to hide pool equipment, leave plenty of space so that damaging chemical spills won't hit the leaves or the soil near the plants.

Chapter Six

Wet Areas

How to make virtue out of necessity

A FEW SPRINGS AGO, I went to see a walkway installed at a home that had been built the summer before. The site looked as if some maniac had systematically taken a backhoe to the formerly smooth and level walk. Stones had heaved and bucked, and for much of the distance to the door, the route lay underwater. The owner blamed frost and faulty walkway construction for the damage.

What had happened had nothing to do with frost or faulty construction. The culprit was the person who graded the lot. He had backfilled around the foundation in a way that led to what landscapers call negative grade—that is, any grade that doesn't move water in the right direction. In this case, water was allowed to flow against the foundation, which not only caused the sidewalk damage, but led to a wet yard and wet basement.

If there is a wet area in the yard, one of three factors probably accounts for it: either the grade is not correct (as the above example demonstrates), the soil is saturated, or there are surfacing underground springs. A wet area is an inconvenience because it's not mowable, and it can be unsightly. So it's important to determine the source of the problem. Then take proper remedial action.

Water in the basement probably means improper outside grading. The law of gravity dictates that if the earth is sloping toward the foundation of a home, water will flow in that direction. The inevitable result is a wet basement.

Underground springs or runoff from another site will create just as much trouble as improper grading, if not more, because the fix is not as straightforward.

But in the case of springs and runoff, there is a silver lining. The homeowner can turn the problem to his or her advantage by making that section of the yard into a serene water garden that will be the envy of high and dry neighbors.

Wet Yard Wet Basement

ALL TOO OFTEN, a cursory backfilling is ordered by the contractor without any attention paid to the rest of the yard. No one takes the time to ensure positive grade. The topsoil is dumped on top of a poor grading job, and the lawn is installed. Water is free to go wherever it chooses, no matter what the consequences.

Proper Grading & Backfilling

I WOULD VENTURE TO SAY that almost every yard I have been to in the past sixteen years has had to be properly graded before any other landscaping could be done. If there is a limited budget, don't skip to the walkways or plantings. Properly grade the yard first. The last thing anyone wants is a wet basement and a yard that is muddy, impossible to maintain and a mosquito breeding ground.

Before you begin, remember the obvious: water runs downhill. Then, make sure any

water you have on your yard has a "hill" down which to run. It needn't be much of an incline. A one-inch drop for every eight feet is sufficient. But don't rely on doing it by eye, which is probably why the problem exists in the first place. Use a transit or construction level to determine the grading plan that will allow the water to flow to where you want it to go. Try to remove the existing ups and downs to establish a smooth, continuous grade.

If there is a city street nearby with gutters and catch basins, it is obvious where to direct the water, but if there are obstacles between the house and the catch basin, the water's route needs to be planned. You

may have to hire or rent a skid steer loader or a tractor with a bucket to adjust the grading.

Think ahead to where the water should flow and create swales (shallow and narrow depressions that catch the water) to channel it properly. Of course, always make sure that there is a positive grade around the foundation of the house. If there are plantings in the way, dig them up, grade the soil, and replant at the new level. Simply burying the plantings to

First, remember the obvious: water runs downhill.
Then, make sure any water you have on your yard has a "hill" down which to run.
The incline need not be great. A one-inch drop for every eight feet is sufficient.
Swales should channel water to a street drain or other run-off area.

---

raise the grade will cause suffocation from the added soil on the roots. Channels and swales should be barely perceptible to the eye. Water will move as long as the ground is not level and

there is an outlet for it to escape.

If you have a choice, the best time to seed in most areas is late summer and early autumn, so if it fits your schedule, plan to get the grading

Three factors account for wet patches in the landscape: either the grade is not correct, the soil is saturated, or an underground spring is surfacing nearby. Whatever the cause, a wet area is an inconvenience because it is not easily mowed and can become unsightly. Determine the source of the problem, then take proper remedial action.

done during those months. In the fall, the lawn will reestablish itself as quickly as possible with the least weed growth. If the work has to be done during the summer, consider sodding the area after the grading to spare yourself the mud. If the original lawn is well established and healthy, use a sod cutter (a rentable machine that uniformly peels the sod away from the ground) to remove the existing sod, grade properly, and lay the original sod back in place. Don't count on being able to cover 100 percent of the disturbed area with the recycled sod, so start with areas closest to the house and other active parts of the yard.

Problem

A Perpetually Wet Area

WHAT HAPPENS IF YOU HAVE made sure the grade in your yard is correct and you are still faced with a corner that refuses to dry out? Chances are that there is an underground spring surfacing. If that is the case, you will either have to drain it or use it to create a pond or other water feature.

In the illustration above, adversity has been turned
to advantage by "going with the flow." Instead of attempting to drain
the permanently wet area beside the driveway, the landscaper has planted trees,
shrubs and perennials that thrive in the moist conditions that originally led
to the cattail-clogged eyesore depicted on the opposite page.

Remedy 1

Underground Drainage

I F GRADING PROBLEMS have been corrected and there is still a wet area, it is safe to bet that there is a spring surfacing in the yard. To make the area dry, underground piping must be used to direct the water to another location. The rule to remember is that if the water is on the surface, use surface grading to remedy the problem; water originating beneath the surface of the ground needs underground drainage for proper correction.

As with all landscape projects, start with a well-thought-out plan. First, establish the ultimate high and low spot in the problem area. Decide where the water should end up. Properly engineered subsurface drainage tiles need to either lead to a street catch basin at the low end, be directed to a dry well, or end in a swale that carries the water away. Then, plot a course for the drain tile from the final point toward the water source. Repeatedly measure the depth to ensure positive grade.

When the digging is finished, move quickly

If you have an underground spring surfacing in your yard,
consider yourself lucky. You have the option of building a pond.
There are many recreational benefits to the backyard pond—swimming, fishing,
and ice skating in the winter, to name a few. Ponds also attract a wide variety of wildlife.
However don't make the mistake of assuming that any wet area can become a pond.
Spend a year observing the proposed pond site to make certain
the wetness is not just a seasonal phenomenon.

because, depending on the soil type and its moisture content, the side walls of the trench may cave in. Go back to the outflow and spread a one-inch layer of one-inch diameter washed stone. Lay the pipe on top of this layer. I suggest using four-inch black plastic field drainage tile that has slotted openings. Spend a few extra dollars and purchase a myrify "sock" to wrap around the tile. The sock ensures against mud seeping in and rendering the tile ineffective. Cover the pipe with a few inches of the washed stone.

Once the stone is installed all the way to the source, the clean-up begins. Replace the soil over the drainage stone to complete the backfilling. Be sure to compact the soil in the trench before sodding or seeding so there will be no settling problems. If the time was taken to strip off the sod first, carefully fit trimmed pieces back together, and cover the trench.

Occasionally, there is an area in the yard where water collects that does not permit proper grading. In such cases, the answer is to install a catch basin. Obtained at plumbing-supply houses, catch basins are cylinders with grates on top and punch-outs on the bottom to accommodate pipes. Install the catch basin in the middle of the low spot to attract the water and dig a properly graded trench to an out-of-harm's-way area or to a street catch basin. In this case, the drainpipe should be solid (without slots).

Remedy 2
Turn Wetness to Your Advantage: Build a Pond

AN UNDERGROUND SPRING isn't always bubbling at the surface. When we needed to install our home water system, we went searching for underground springs using indicator plants as clues. Certain plants will only survive if their roots are near a water source. Stands of arborvitae or "trees of life" (eastern white cedar) are primary indicator plants, because if they are growing wild, it is sure there is a spring beneath them. Similarly, willows, poplars and larches inhabit wet soils. Other obvious indicator plants are cattails, sedges and purple loosestrife. If you do have a spring, consider yourself lucky. You are a candidate to have a pond on your property. There are many recreational uses for ponds like swimming, fishing and ice skating, but don't overlook the benefit of attracting wildlife and creating a sanctuary for both your family and water-loving animals. A word of caution: be sure to check local and state ordinances before disturbing existing wetlands.

Prior to construction, make a plan and realize that there is more to pond building than digging a hole. Some basic components are necessary to end up with a successful living pond rather than a seasonal mosquito ranch. The key is a constant and consistent water source. Don't make the mistake of thinking that just because a low spot on the property is wet every spring it will support a year-round pond site. One of the things I recommend is to spend a full year observing the proposed pond site regularly, noting where the sources of water appear to be and when the area dries out.

Although the most attractive ponds are those that closely mimic nature,
a solid plan is still necessary because pond construction is one project that is not easily
altered to accommodate future whims. The excavator should include nooks and crannies,
rather than dig a simple oval or square shape. Also incorporate such features as docks,
beaches and piers into the plan. Overhanging trees like weeping willows,
together with smaller shoreline plants, contribute to a natural look.

If the area stays soggy, even during the driest months of the year, it's probably an ideal site, as long as the presence of water is not just the result of a heavy clay soil harboring seasonal runoff.

Another way to test the water source is to dig a hole at its low point during the driest part of the year and place a five-gallon pail in the bottom of it to catch the water. Pump the hole dry, if possible, and measure the flow by timing how long it takes for the bucket to refill. Then calculate the gallons-per-minute flow. Once the pond is filled from seasonal runoff, enough flow is needed to keep up with evaporation, plus it should compensate for a slight but constant outflow of water. The more water movement, the better the aeration and the healthier the pond.

Excavating a Pond

BUT FLOWING WATER ALONE is not enough for a successful pond. The soil must be heavy enough to support it. Light, gravelly or sandy soil that drains easily is not adequate. That problem must be alleviated by lining the bottom and sides of the excavated hole with at least a foot of heavy clay soil, an added expense.

Whatever the condition of the soil, heavy machinery is required to dig the hole for the pond. We usually hire a competent subcontractor with a bulldozer and backhoe. The shape and size of the pond are dependent on potential uses and location. I prefer a natural look with nooks and crannies to a perfectly oval man-made appearance.

Again, a plan is necessary for complete satisfaction, because this is one project that is not easily altered to accommodate future whims. Some ideas to incorporate into the basic pond design are decks, gazebos or fishing piers. All require advance consideration because posts must be inserted in the pond bottom before it fills with water.

Determine how the deck will be used before deciding what shape or size it should be. Choose an area of the pond for your deck where the water depth is adequate for diving even if diving is not going to be allowed. The pond's bottom must be free of all debris and rocks near the deck. If a deck is planned for an existing pond, the pond will need to be drained most of the way to install posts, so clean up the bottom at that time. There is no excuse for neglecting to make the area safe around the deck or docks.

If the plan is to support fish, successful overwintering is a major concern in colder areas, and adequate depth may play a key role. Setting up the delicate ecosystem necessary for some species of fish may require shelves incorporated into the pond floor for aquatic plants. Growing aquatics in tubs on shelves keeps them from invading the whole pond as well as placing them at the proper height.

Drainpipes & Spillways

ANOTHER IMPORTANT PIECE of the pond engineering puzzle is having a correctly constructed and installed drainpipe. The type we use consists of a riser pipe (whose diameter is dependent on the amount of water that's needed to flow out of the pond) that stands vertically in the pond as tall as the desired water level. The riser is connected to a horizontal pipe (called the barrel), roughly twice the diameter of the riser. The barrel is set so that the outfall end is inserted through the wall of the pond (dike) and drains without jeopardizing the integrity of the pond by erosion. A low spot should be left in the top of the pond dike, approximately six inches higher than the top of the drain riser, to allow for an emergency spillway in the case of heavy runoff or rainfall.

To make the pond more accessible, consider building a beach. Again, it's best to do this before the pond has completely filled. First, decide how large an area to maintain, because as with any artificially constructed feature, a man-made beach will not last forever without upkeep. Scrape away any grass, weeds and soil to a depth of a foot in the prospective beach area. Spread four to six inches of clean peastone over the area, and cover the top of the stone with woven weed-barrier cloth (myrify fabric), generously overlapping the seams. Finally, spread the remainder of the excavated depth with clean beach or masonry sand. Compact the entire surface with a plate compactor or roller.

Those who feel that a pond project is too big can still capitalize on a wet area by building a waterfall, brook or reflecting pool. In building a brook, the hardest part of the task is making something that looks natural for its entire length. Be sure to include rocks, native plants and trees to reduce the feeling of artificiality.

Remedy 3

Go with the Flow: Construct a Small Water Feature

IF A POND PROJECT IS TOO GRAND, there are other, smaller-scale water features that can be built. Capitalize on existing springs by creating a waterfall, brook or reflecting pool.

For me, the hardest part is creating a water feature that looks natural for its entire length.

It's easy enough, with some imagination, to make a natural-looking brook, but not so easy to give it a source and an end that don't look contrived, especially in an urban neighborhood. Planning and designing should be carefully executed to include native trees, shrubs and perennials that are integrated into the grand scheme of the lot's landscaping. An isolated water feature without the softening of plants will look like it belongs on a false-fronted Hollywood set.

An existing spring may not provide enough flow to create what you want, but you can supplement the water with a recirculating pump that is inexpensive, safe and easy to install. Recirculating pumps can be used even if there is no source of water. Instead of piping away the excess at the end of the feature, recirculate all the water within it.

With an existing spring, it is obvious where the water feature will be located, but it may not be obvious how to start. If a waterfall or brook is desired, some elevation must be added to cause the water to move in a specified direction. For a natural appearance, an artificial brook should meander, though not necessarily in a far-reaching way. Create a pool at the top of the falls or brook and one at the end. With a natural spring, the bottom pool should have an underground outlet to take the water away.

The pools and channels should be lined with flexible plastic, rigid preformed plastic or concrete. With smaller projects, it is simplest and most reliable to use a flexible plastic liner. Heavy-gauge black-colored butyl is the preferred material. Although concrete can be shaped to look natural, there is more risk of cracking and leakage.

The next step is to begin excavation. The water source will need to be diverted until the excavation and construction is complete. Start from the bottom by shaping the pool. Gently slope the banks away from the center and make shelves for rocks and aquatic plants.

Keep in mind that some plants, particularly lilies, prefer quiet water. Form shelves for potted lilies 15 to 24 inches below the water's surface. Most water lilies will grow within that range quite successfully. Some need more depth (up to 36 inches). Plant water lilies in containers for two reasons. The first is that some are not hardy enough to survive a northern winter, so removal to a greenhouse or other warm area when the cold weather threatens will be necessary. The other is that they are so prolific that if left on their own, they will quickly fill the entire pool, choke out other plants and foul the water.

Build the brooks or waterfalls from the lowest end up. If the yard does not naturally slope, pay attention to grading. You may have to build up an area to accommodate the feature.

Regardless of whether a small water feature is to be formal or natural, once excavation is complete, it is necessary to line the bottom and sides with a material like butyl. Rocks and edging will hold down the liner. Shelves at various depths should be included to accommodate potted aquatic plants like irises and water lilies.

*Filled and fully operational, the reflecting pool under construction on the previous page
has become a place of serenity and beauty. The edges can support a wide variety of moisture-loving
perennials like ferns, irises, hostas and grasses. As they grow, a lush, full effect is achieved
by allowing their foliage to hang over the side.*

Hide the unnaturalness of it with plantings and boulders, but remember only one inch of pitch in eight feet of drop is needed to make water flow, so don't go overboard. The brisker the flow, the louder the water. Peaceful, gently flowing water may be more your style.

Once excavation is complete, line the earth with butyl, concrete, or rigid plastic. The rigid preformed plastic is most suitable for the pool areas, but it limits choices for the shape

of the pool and may not include shelves for plants or rocks or have the depth required for some plants and fish. That's why I like the flexibility of butyl liners. Just remember to overlap the liner if more than one sheet is used, with the uppermost sheet lying over the next, which is over the next, and so on.

Engineering and installing the piping and pumping scheme should be done at this point. Once the system is in place and it has been tested for success, it's time

Water Lily

to start naturalizing and beautifying your water feature. When it comes to this task, rocks are a landscaper's best friends. They hold down and camouflage the liner. Rocks also channel and contain the water. Typically, I line the entire creek bed and its edges with rocks. I choose special ones for the spillways, leaving a lip for the water to fall over. If the rocks are not even, I shim them with smaller pieces to position and tilt them properly. It is always best to avoid positioning the rocks in a row if you are trying to achieve a natural effect. For the same reason, try to use rocks that are indigenous to the area or at least are all the same geologic type. Mixing rock types will look artificial.

Line the edges of the water feature with moisture-loving perennials like ferns, irises, grasses and hostas. I try to place the plants so that their foliage will hang over the rocks and follow the meandering course of the water. That produces a lush, full effect useful in naturalizing the feature and hiding its sides. Moving away from the waterfall, pool or brook, graduate the size of the plants to create a layered landscape that will blend with the rest of the yard.

Although some leaf drop can't be helped, try to avoid having a water feature inundated with leaves. A cover can be placed over the area in the autumn to be removed in spring if fish are not overwintering there. A screen should be used if there are fish in the pool. A huge build-up of organic matter like leaves on the bottom of the water feature will eventually foul the water with methane gas.

In addition to water lilies, certain iris varieties, marsh marigolds (*Caltha palustris*), and miniature cattails (*Typha minima*) will grow in the water. They, too, should be planted in rich compost and confined in pots or crates or they will clog a small pool.

Some plants actually help to oxygenate the water, which is critical for healthy fish. For

Water Lily

this reason, it is best for the plants to become established before introducing the fish. The most common oxygenators are Canadian pond weed (*Elodea canadensis*), water milfoil (*Myriophyllum verticillatum*), and water crowfoot (*Ranunculus aquatilis*), all available through mail-order catalogues. They will arrive unrooted in bunches ready for sticking into pots. Often they have lead weights around their bases to hold them in the planting media until they're established.

There are also floating plants that help shade the water for fish, provide food and discourage algae growth. Many species are too prolific for small pools, but two worth trying are ivy-leaved duckweed (*Lemna trisulca*) and water-soldier (*Stratiotes aloides*), which floats under the water's surface until it rises and blooms, sinking again to the bottom where it overwinters.

There are several species of water lilies (*Nymphaea*) both hardy and tropical, all needing full sun. A few particularly suited to small pools are 'Pink Opal' and 'Mary Patricia', both light pink cultivars; 'Ellisiana' and 'James Brydon', both reds and very adaptable; white pygmy (*N. pygmaea* 'Alba'), a small white species; and 'Helvola' and 'Graziella', the former being canary yellow and the latter, copper-colored. All the above species and hybrids keep their spreading growth to a minimum, usually bloom throughout the summer and are ideal for pot culture because of their size and depth requirements.

There are two types of lily roots: one is a thick tuber that looks like a potato, and the other consists of fleshy rhizomes. Plant both types with the crown or top of the root just peeking through the surface of the soil, but lay the rhizomatous root horizontally in the soil and insert the tuberous root vertically. Use rich, well-composted soil in the pots or crates and place newly planted pots on blocks or bricks until the lilies have grown to their full size. Keep removing bricks as they grow. Lilies will be at their best in the second year and should be divided every three to four years in the spring. It's time to divide when the leaves no longer lay flat on the water's surface.

Remedy 4
Wetland Plantings

IF A WETLAND LENDS ITSELF to neither drainage nor construction of a pond or water feature, there are many moisture-loving native plants that will not only enhance the area but will serve to attract wildlife with colorful flowers and berries. In fact, with the right mix of plants, trees and shrubs, what was once an unattractive, hard-to-maintain eyesore can become one of the most pleasant

corners of the yard. The key is to select plants that thrive in wet areas.

When most home landscapers envision plants for wet areas, they either think of the very tall—willows, silver maples—or the very short—irises, marsh marigolds. What gets overlooked is the wonderful array of mid-sized moisture-loving shrubs that are not only as well adapted to wetland settings as their taller and shorter counterparts, but add beauty, interest and texture that could make your wet area the envy of your neighbors.

Moisture-Loving Shrubs

Andromeda polifolia (bog rosemary) is extremely hardy, mostly evergreen, and perfect as an edging plant because of its small size (ultimately two feet high by three feet wide). Bog rosemary likes peaty soil and a cool, moist atmosphere similar to the bog conditions in which it grows naturally. It has very dark green foliage and light pink flowers in the spring. In a layered planting, use this sun-loving or light-shade plant with looser-growing, soft-textured shrubs behind it because its habit tends to be stiff and upright.

Native rhododendrons mix well with bog rosemary. *Rhododendron viscosum* (swamp aza-

Marsh Marigold

Moisture-loving plants not only enhance a wet area, but they attract wildlife with their colorful flowers and berries. Supporting the right mix of tall, mid-sized and ground-hugging plants, a hard-to-maintain trouble spot can be transformed into one of the most pleasant corners of the yard.

lea) has a loose habit and varies in size, growing from two to six feet in height and spreading as wide. Swamp azalea has white spring flowers that are spice-scented and prefers the acid, peaty, sandy soils of its cousin, *Rhododendron maximum* (rosebay rhododendron). Rosebay rhododendron grows much larger than swamp azalea, as much as 12 to 15 feet tall, but it shares the same loose, open habit. It prefers more shade, and bears large evergreen leaves as a result. Rosebay's pink flowers are showy from northern New England sites to as far down the eastern United States as South Carolina and Georgia. Another extremely hardy rhododendron, *Rhododendron canadense* (rhodora), is worth a try because of its early spring bright purple flowers. It stays small, about three feet high, is deciduous, and prefers the wet soils of swampy areas. A southern native, *Rhododendron prunifolium* (plum-leaved azalea), is distinctive because its red blooms arrive in midsummer. Plum-leaved azalea prefers sandy, moist soils and grows to 10 feet in height.

Another plant that is a member of the family Ericaceae like rhododendrons is Labrador tea (*Ledum groenlandicum*). It is best grown in the front of layered plantings because it reaches only three feet and spreads as much. Labrador tea adapts to sun or shade, but likes moist, peaty soils. It is quite hardy, slow-growing and evergreen with a round shape, and blooms with showy white flowers in the late spring. Its distant cousin, the American cranberry (*Vaccinium macrocarpon*), has beautiful dark green, glossy foliage that stays evergreen and spreads as a ground cover. American cranberry needs full sun and moist sphagnum to keep its roots cool. It only reaches six inches in height, so the front of the border is a perfect location to show off the bright red fruits we all enjoy at Thanksgiving. A close relative, the highbush blueberry (*Vaccinium corymbosum*), also provides wildlife and humans with a bounty of berries in the fall and is native to swampy sites requiring acid, humusy soils. It will reach 12 feet and become 10 feet wide, so allow space.

Summer Scents

FOR MIDSUMMER blooming and spicy scent, try *Clethra alnifolia* (summersweet), a little known four- to eight-foot deciduous shrub that bears extremely fragrant white or pink flowers in the middle of the summer. Some people don't consider the long, spiky flowers to be that showy, but it's impossible to pass by *Clethra* without noticing it because of its scent. *Clethra* is pest-free and one of the best plants for shade and wet conditions. It is happy in acid, humusy soils as well as salty seashore sites. Another little-known deciduous shrub that forms a thick ground cover about two feet high is *Xanthorhiza simplicissima* (shrub yellow-root). In

Winterberry

a shady, wet site, yellow-root will completely cover the front border. The leaves of yellow-root look like those of celery, with long, fringed leaflets clustered on the branches. Its common name is derived from the yellow dye Native Americans distilled from the sap of the plant. Similar to *Clethra* in flowering appearance and not commonly used, a good small (five feet) deciduous shrub for southern New England to Florida is *Itea virginica* (Virginia sweetspire). Its red fall color is spectacular, and the fragrant white six-inch-long and spiky flowers bloom in the middle of summer in the North and the spring in the South. *Itea* is adaptable to sun or shade.

The genus *Cornus,* of which the well-known flowering dogwood is a part, contains a few wetland species as well. Very hardy *Cornus sericea* (red twig dogwood) grows fast to eight feet or so, but is most distinctive because of its red twigs which brighten in the fall and winter and look striking against the white snow. Its four-season appeal really looks best when several are planted together as a mass. Yellow-stemmed dogwood, cultivar 'Flaviramea', gives a similar colorful effect. Silky dogwood, *Cornus amomum*, is a medium-growing shrub (about six feet high and wide) that produces an interesting blue and white fruit that birds love. Silky dogwood does well in sun or shade, but prefers the edge of the swamp.

THE HOLLY, a familiar sight at holiday time, has cousins that do well in the home landscape. *Ilex verticillata* (winterberry), *I. glabra* (inkberry), and *I. vomitoria* (yaupon) are native to wet lowlands and produce a profusion of berries that vary from black to red. One caveat: hollies need male and female shrubs planted near each other to produce berries.

One of my favorite families of plants for the middle of moist-area plantings are the viburnums. Typically, they have white flowers and good fall color. Some, like *Viburnum plicatum* 'Mariesii' (double file), have unusual horizontal branching habits and others, like *V. carlesii* (Koreanspice), have very fragrant flowers. While all like moist soils, *V. opulus* (European cranberry bush) thrives in wet, boggy areas. It is a large deciduous shrub, 12 feet by 12 feet, and likes sun. *V. opulus* usually turns red in the fall and produces clusters of red berries. Although it can be pestered by aphids, it makes a good show at the middle to rear of the layered wetland planting.

Trees for Wet Areas

IF TALLER TREE-HEIGHT is preferred, there are many common species like green ash, sycamore and arborvitae from which to choose.

For interesting deciduous texture and great height (up to 75 feet), the European larch (*Larix decidua*) has wonderful yellow-orange fall color. Larch need sun and wet soils to perform best, and the uninformed would swear they are an evergreen tree because of their needlelike leaves.

Also prominent for fall foliage color are a few of the maples that like wet feet: *Acer saccharinum* (silver maple) and *A. rubrum* (red or swamp maple). I include silver maple more as a caution than as a recommendation. It is typically one of the most requested trees in a garden center because of its silver-bottomed leaves and fast growth habit. But silver maple is short-lived because it is so fast-growing. It becomes weak wooded, self-destructing in the wind and snow, but is useful for screening and shade while a slower-growing, better tree is getting established. Very hardy and up to 75 feet in height, silver maple is best planted where its roots won't intrude and ruin concrete or underground piping and pond walls. It will survive a complete inundation of water, and may be one of the best choices where seasonal flooding occurs. On the other hand, *A. rubrum* is a fine species for outstanding early red fall color and attractive-looking primordial leaves in the spring. It's not as fast a grower as silver maple and stays a bit smaller, in the 50-foot range. Many cultivars have been developed that produce richer fall color and more upright form, but my experience in growing red maple (not to be confused with crimson king maple, which has red leaves all season long) is that the seedling of a straight species growing on its own root (as opposed to a grafted cultivar) is hardiest. Another feature of red maple is its early flowers that truly serve as a beacon of spring for those of us in the far North who need assurance that spring will come.

Two of the easiest-to-grow oaks that specifically enjoy wet areas are *Quercus palustris* (pin oak) and *Q. nigra* (water oak). Pin oak grows as well in northern Vermont as in southern gardens. It's a large sun-loving tree (75 to 100 feet) and survives city conditions, although pin oak is native to wet clay flats filled with seasonal standing water. Excellent red fall color and a horizontal branching habit are characteristic of pin oak. Water oak only grows as far north as New Jersey, has a round head and narrow, unlobed leaves. The dried leaves hang on into the winter, which make oaks good candidates for pondside and other water feature plantings where dead leaves may clog drainpipes and contaminate the water.

N O WETLAND PLANT DESCRIPTIONS would be complete without the willows. The graceful weeping willow (*Salix alba* 'Niobe') makes a striking impact where space is no object, however beware the "dirtiness" of this tree. Every gust of the wind drops leaves and branches. Goat willow (*Salix caprea*) is commonly known as pussy willow because of the softness of the catkin. It reaches 15 to 20 feet in height and flowers early in the spring. A most interesting willow to try is *Salix elaeagnos* (rosemary willow), because its leaves are very similar to the herb rosemary: long, narrow and dark green. Manageable in size as a six- to eight-foot shrub, rosemary willow loves wetness and is inclined to grow densely.

Perennial Plants for a Wet Area

S EVERAL PERENNIALS are appropriate for wetland plantings. Some prefer just moist soils while others will tolerate short periods of standing water.

For moist edges and modest amounts of standing water, irises head the list. Japanese iris (*Iris kaempferi or I. ensata*) grows two to three feet high and flowers blue or purple with

Weeping Willow

Japanese Iris

a contrasting white color. Variegated rabbitear iris (*I. laevigata* 'Variegata') is shorter than Japanese iris, about 18 to 24 inches tall, has blue flowers and a white stripe in the leaf. Both irises must have wet soils, but Japanese prefer acid soil and rabbitear will accept basic soil.

Another marsh-loving plant, this one in the buttercup family, marsh marigold (*Caltha palustris*) has two-inch yellow flowers and heart-shaped leaves. Best grown in clumps, *Caltha* blooms first thing in the spring.

Wet soil by the water's edge is beautifully graced by bog arum (*Calla palustris*) at eight inches high. The plants are covered by small, white arum-shaped flowers with orange centers in early summer. The orange spiky centers become red spikes of berries in the fall if they are pollinated by water snails.

Many wetland perennials have interesting foliage with inconspicuous or unconventional-looking flowers. Sweet flag is a member of the genus *Acorus,* which has two-foot irislike foliage that, when bruised, gives off a tangerine scent. Other plants to consider for their foliage are *Juncus effusus* var. *spiralis* (corkscrew rush), *Cyperus* species (sedges), and *Sagittaria sagittifolia* (old-world arrowhead). True to its name, corkscrew rush twists and turns on 18-inch

Astilbe

stems while the sedges' stems are flat-sided, sharp and, usually, grasslike. As my botany professor said, "Sedges have edges." Arrowheads are 18 inches tall and serve as oxygenating plants as they sit in shallow water at pond's edge. Along with the arrow-shaped foliage, the spiky white flowers have black and red centers.

A Primrose Primer

SOME OF THE BEST PLANTS for the bog garden are in the primrose family. The bog primulas generally have leaves at the base and flowers that form a whorl (circle) around the upper stem. A few worthy of note are *Primula beesiana,* with fragrant purple flowers in early summer; the early flowering *P. denticulata,* with large lavender flowers on 12-inch stems; and the giant cowslip, *P. florindae*, sporting yellow bell-shaped, fragrant and nodding early-summer flowers. The leaves of *P. florindae* are huge, and the entire plant can reach three feet in height.

Lobelia cardinalis, or cardinal flower, loves wet soils. With its riot of scarlet flowers in summer, *L. cardinalis* is very tall, three or four feet, and prefers a shaded site. Many other moist-soil perennials like shade as well. *Aruncus dioicus* (goatsbeard) is in the rose family. Its creamy flowers appear like feathers floating above the foliage. *Astilbe*, shorter and ranging in flower shades from cream to pink to red, has similar foliage and flower shape to *Aruncus*. A favorite *Astilbe* of mine is *A. rosea* 'Peach Blossom' with its strong scent. I also love *A. tacquetii* 'Superba' that blooms rose-red for a long period each summer.

A low growing semi-evergreen with large heart-shaped tropical-looking leaves, *Bergenia cordifolia* provides a wonderful texture change in perennial gardens. In the early spring, pink flowers rise on a short stem from the clump's center, while the leaves spread in a circular pattern around them. My shady, moist border has *Bergenia* at the front with a huge *Hosta sieboldiana elegans* behind them. Hostas, or plantain lilies, range in size from dwarf four-inch-tall specimens to monstrous ones four or five feet in diameter. There are 40 known species with many variations of leaf color: blues, yellows, whites and greens. Some species are colored at the edges of their leaves, some are blotchy in the center; some are crinkled like seersucker, some are smooth and shiny. Lavender, white or violet flowers shoot up from the center on tall stems in mid to late summer. Hostas are perfect for edging along man-made or natural water features. The foliage softens rocks and provides a skirt for the front of a layered planting. A few interesting, yet not uncommon varieties worth mentioning are *H. undulata*, with wavy green leaves with white stripes, and *H. sieboldiana* 'Frances Williams', with huge, seersucker yellow-edged blue leaves.

Another giant, unusual-looking perennial is *Ligularia* x *przewalskii* 'The Rocket', which loves shady, wet and bog conditions. The huge, heart-shaped leaves stay low on the plant, have a gray-green cast, and are sharply toothed all around. Tall, four-foot, dark stems bear yellow flowers in long spikes. *Ligularia* is a striking plant especially when massed in the shade at water's edge.

Too Much of a Good Thing

THERE ARE A FEW moisture-loving plants that should be used with caution because of their invasive nature. Purple loosestrife (*Lythrum salicaria*) makes an impressive show in wet lowlands along roadsides, but, let loose, will clog and mire a garden pond, choking out other native plants. Use the loosestrife cultivars like red-flowered 'Robert' and pink-flowering 'Happy' to avoid the problem. *Phalaris arundinacea* var. *picta*, or gardener's garters, is in the grass family, does well where other plants may find the conditions too harsh, and has white and pink variegated foliage. But it, too, will spread with a passion. Controlled growth is necessary for members of the genus *Typha*, the cattails. The brown bottle brushes are actually female flowers that have a cream-colored group of male flowers above them. When left to their own devices, cattails quickly spread and choke a pond. To contain loosestrife and cattails, grow them in barrels buried in the ground.

Chapter Seven

Shady Dealings

Landscaping where the sun doesn't shine

L IKE ANIMALS, PLANTS ADAPT to changes in their surroundings in order to survive. Those that cannot respond suffer and may die. Certain plant species have evolved to live in the shade, and because of specific characteristics of adaptation, prefer that environment. Plants that grow in the shade tend to have larger, thinner leaves to provide a broader surface for photosynthesis to occur and because the chloroplasts, or cells that carry chlorophyll, are oriented horizontally in the leaf rather than piled on top of each other, as in sun-loving plants. Put them in the light and their leaves will burn.

Adjustment to low light conditions is only one of the adaptations shade-loving plants have made. Because many low-light plants occur naturally in the understory of the woods, they prefer moist, rich, humusy soils as well as shade.

The ecology of the woods is not quickly or easily reproduced in a yard any more than a sunny, dry meadow could be created under the spreading branches of a stand of mature hardwoods. So I suggest building on what the habitat of the existing yard is like. Use sun-loving plants in the open, high areas, wet-loving plants in the lowlands, drought-tolerant plants where it's dry, and shade-loving plants where the light and environment are suitable.

Problem

Shady Yard, Sparse Lawn

GRASS, FOR THE MOST PART, simply is not adapted to life in the shade. Try as you might to grow it, a good stand of grass in a shady area is a virtual impossibility. I know there are grass-seed bags with lettering screaming: SHADE MIX. What they don't scream is: maybe, under perfect growing conditions—the right blend of soil pH (acid or basic), water and nutrients.

In a shady yard, the growing conditions are usually far from perfect for grass. Often, the presence of large trees, especially evergreens, decreases the pH and nutrient levels of the soil to such a degree that few grasses will tolerate it. Thick piles of decaying organic matter from the forest floor can play havoc with plants except those that are used to being part of the understory and the conditions of that ecosystem. The presence of moss is a good indicator of the presence of acidic soils lawns dislike. Digging it out or using a moss eradicator is a band-aid that will not remedy the problem.

Of course, trees are not the only cause of shade in a yard. Nearby buildings can have the same effect. For this reason, the north side of many houses is perpetually shady.

Instead of considering the shady side of the house a messy-looking liability where grass won't grow and people won't sit, take advantage of the moist, cool conditions and create a lush, thriving shade garden in which visitors and family members will want to linger.

Remedy 1

Improve the Soil

I SUGGEST IMPROVING THE SOIL in the shady parts of any yard, but it's a particularly good idea if the shady area did not exist before the house was built. The humus-rich soils of most natural shade environments take years to build up. To replicate them, normal soils must be augmented with compost. Composting household scraps, leaves and grass clippings is not only convenient but is an environmentally sound practice. Choose a sunny, out-of-the-way spot (but convenient to the kitchen year-round, and to the garden) for the compost pile, bin or heap. There are several manufactured bins available from mail-order supply and gardening houses, but there is no need to be fancy about it.

All organic materials will break down or compost, but avoid bones, large branches, construction debris and prunings from garden plants unless there is absolute certainty they are not diseased. The moist, warm composting environment can be just the fuel some diseases need to proliferate. Do include grass clippings, wood chips and sawdust in the compost pile rather than applying them directly to the flower bed, because as they break down, they rob precious nitrogen from the soil. The addition of manure or commercial fertilizers is necessary to make a nutritive compost heap.

Natural composting is a slow process, so pick a site where more than one pile can be made with one always available for use and where the piles can be left for years.

Heap the organic waste to about six inches, then place a two-inch layer of soil and soil mixed with fertilizer or manure on top of the waste. Always make the layers concave to collect water, as humidity is one of the essentials for composting activity. Repeat the layers un-

The north side of a house is often faceless and stark. Growing options are usually far from perfect for grass. The presence of trees not only diminishes sunlight, but decreases the soil's pH and nutrient levels. Thick piles of decaying leaves can play havoc with any plant not adapted to life in the forest understory.

Instead of considering the shady side of a house a liability, use it to your advantage. The moist, cool conditions are perfect for a lush garden. Shade-loving plants, such as hostas, are layered with taller plants to mimic nature, but care has been taken not to plant too close to the house. Moisture retained there by the plants can cause mildew and rot.

til they are four to five feet high, making sure they are concave. Leave the heap to the elements of nature, and in two or three years it will be ready for use.

To speed the process, turn the pile with a pitchfork once a month. Always put the more solid wastes toward the center so that the composting process will continue. Material in the pile will heat up in the center (to as much as 150 degrees F) while it is decomposing. During that phase, the heat will eliminate any soil-borne plant diseases—an important reason to allow the compost to mature before using it.

Remedy 2
Plant a Shade Garden

DESIGNING A SHADE GARDEN is a bit more involved than planning one for a sunny landscape. All the basic design elements are the same: creative use of texture, color, balance and composition. But most shade gardens are informal because they usually simulate nature's design. The informality of asymmetry capitalizes on the imperfect growth patterns of the forest whose plants are subject to animal "pruning" and breakage from wind.

Shade gardens should be lush and full with meandering paths supplied for human access. A stepping-stone pathway with a prostrate ground cover like *Sagina subulata* (Irish moss) nestled between the stones makes a subtle inroad among the other plantings.

Shade gardens should take full advantage of reduced visual capacity by enhancing other senses. A quiet, pensive space with a bench or hammock allows for reading, listening to wind rustling in the leaves and napping. Most shade flowers aren't bright and colorful. Instead, nature has concentrated on whites and pastels, which become delightful accents in a shady

spot and often deploy fragrances to attract passing insects and birds. Layering the plantings will best mimic nature's way while covering space that would be exposed to weed seeds, erosion and dryness.

Plenty of moisture is necessary for most shade-loving plants. Ground covers are a vital component, because they hold moisture in the ground around the larger trees and shrubs. If a shade garden is to be near a home's foundation, it's particularly important to keep in mind the shade plants' need for moisture. The garden should not be too close to the walls of the house, because the foundation is warmer and drier than shade plants prefer and poor air circulation will promote mildew growth. Island beds, wide enough for layered planting, may be more prudent and will help fill the space taken up by a less-than-perfect lawn.

If your yard boasts a naturally wooded section, consider yourself lucky, for a large number of attractive shade-loving plants will find themselves at home there and nowhere else.

Be sure to plant in a wooded area with the seasons in mind. Before the leaves open fully on deciduous trees, the garden will be sunny and perfect for the spring colors of daffodils and minor bulbs like grape hyacinths, crocuses and snowdrops. My backyard is completely wooded *and* is situated on the north side of my house, a shade gardener's dream come true. First thing in the spring, the daffodil and crocus show is a real sight. Waves of different-colored daffodils open in succession, extending the season until the last tree leaf in the grove has unfurled. A short pause for the yellow-green of nature's spring colors gives way to azaleas, rhododendrons and ferns interspersed in the understory. Then, many different colors and variegations of hosta foliage seemingly evolve before our eyes until they bloom during the summer. Finally, the autumn sparkle of yellow, orange and red dresses the canopy un-

Be sure to plant a wooded area with the seasons in mind. In early spring,
before the leaves open fully on deciduous trees, the garden will be sunny and perfect for
daffodils and other bulbs like grape hyacinths, crocuses and snowdrops.

til it carpets the floor. Winter, though stark, is a twist and turn of sculptural wonder as the dark trees are silhouetted with snow-coated branches.

Although a natural feeling is preferable for a wooded garden, it doesn't hurt to give nature a hand here and there. I suggest remov-ing some of the understory plants existing in the woods and raising the height of some of the lower tree limbs. Plot the existing trees on a piece of graph paper and remove the undesirable, the dead and the broken. Create a serpentine path winding through the trees to a focal point like a bench, sculpture or interest-

ing tree or shrub. Next, choose medium-sized shrubs in the four- to six-foot range that will provide the second layer of plants. Then, for the third layer, plant dwarf shade lovers of 18 inches to three feet in height. Finally, mass the ground covers and other perennials along the path and under the larger plantings. Start with moderate-sized shrubs, keeping in mind that the moist, cool environment will produce tremendous growth in a relatively short period of time.

It looks most natural to mass the plantings in odd numbers, so begin with groupings of at least three or five, which can be expanded in another season or year. Mix evergreens with deciduous shrubs. Mingle plants that have pointed, elongated leaves with those that have rounder leaves. Combine plants that bear spiked flowers with those that have daisylike blossoms.

Color combinations are fun to experiment with, especially when variegated foliage is considered a part of the overall color scheme. There's no worry about clashing when using perennial shade-loving plants, as mostly whites and pastels will be at hand. Occasionally, a hot pink rhododendron or orange azalea will perk up the design. Annuals like impatiens, coleus and tuberous begonias are full of pizzazz, while warmer-climate perennials like camellias and caladiums add wonderful color opportunities. (In cooler climates, these perennials should be treated as annual bulbs.) Two of my favorite ground covers are *Lamium maculatum* 'White Nancy', with its tinfoil-like sparkling leaves, and *Pulmonaria,* or lungwort, the white polka-dotted green-leaved ground cover with early mixed pink and blue flowers. Both have striking foliage that is absolutely brilliant in the shade. My experience has been that in the filtered light of the shade, reds seem to get redder, blues bluer and whites whiter. The Japanese maple on the north side of my house on the fringe of the woods has bright crimson leaves all summer, but in the fall, its red color is unsurpassed.

Dig carefully when working around tree roots, because it is easy to injure the small feeders that absorb water and nutrients from the soil. It's best to give shrubs plenty of distance from the existing trees so that moisture will not be trapped against the trunks of the trees and roots will not be harmed in the digging process. Airflow is important to the health of the plants.

It is also a good idea to have a soil test done before selecting plants, so that the best conditions can be provided. Rhododendrons and many other broadleaf evergreens prefer acidic soils, which are common in the woods, but low pH may not be suitable for some plants.

MANY SHADE-LOVING PLANTS are also suited to moist areas because shade and moisture usually go hand in hand. Shade lovers are the fringe plantings in the wetland garden, because most won't tolerate standing water. Native species dominate the shade lovers, but many have been hybridized for superior characteristics like smaller size, insect and disease resistance, larger flower size with better color, and foliage shape, color and texture.

A well-designed shade garden incorporates a mixture of trees, shrubs, perennials and ground covers. A good plan with four-season appeal should include the earliest of spring flowers as well as the sculptural interest of bare branches for winter.

Harbingers of Spring

ONE OF THE FIRST deciduous beacons of spring is shadbush (*Amelanchier*). While the last of the snow is piled along the roadsides, shadbush's white flowers peek through the other trees to the edges of the woods. A partial shade lover, downy serviceberry, or juneberry (*A. arborea*), grows to about 20 feet, and its white spring flowers become black berries in early summer. *A. canadensis* is a little smaller (six to ten feet) blooms a little bit later, has golden fall color and very sweet, juicy, black fruit. Allegheny serviceberry (*A. laevis*) differs in that the opening leaves are a bronze color. The shads attract many forms of wildlife because of their berries, but the human appeal is their flowers—a sure sign that spring has arrived. No shade planting is complete without a few shads tucked into edges of the border.

Even earlier blooming than shad is deciduous vernal witch hazel (*Hamamelis vernalis*). Witch hazel is a real tease because, even in the north, it blooms in late January or February,

Northern Bayberry

withstanding low temperatures by rolling its petals up protectively from the cold. The usually yellow (sometimes red) fragrant flowers, borne on six- to ten-foot gray stems, last about three weeks. A little hardier is *H. virginiana*, the common witch hazel. It is a much larger shrub, up to 30 feet high and as wide. Since it is so large, common witch hazel should only be used on sites that will accommodate its size. It flowers in the very late fall, from October to early December, a most unusual time for blooming. Chinese witch hazel (*H. mollis*) is less hardy than its counterparts, blooms in the very early spring with yellow flowers and is more manageable in size at ten feet high. It's outstanding for its flower fragrance and yellow to orange fall leaf color. The witch hazels bring flowers at odd times, but should only be chosen as additions to the shade garden if native, woody, very large shrubs will fit the scheme.

Myrica pensylvanica (Northern bayberry) should be in every shade garden. Bayberry adapts to most any soil type and has a natural, perfect shape: upright but rounded. The leaves are shiny dark green and give off a spicy aroma when crushed. The gray-powder-coated berries are closely held near the stem and last the winter through. I consider bayberry to be a fine, stately middle-of-the-border shrub as long as it is easily seen and admired for its habit. At only three feet, *Comptonia peregrina* (sweet fern) complements bayberry because it spreads wide, but also has very aromatic dark green foliage. The leaves are similar to those of a fern—long and many-lobed—looking quite at home in the woodland garden.

The Viburnum Clan

AS DIVERSE A GROUP of deciduous shade lovers as can be found is the viburnum clan. I have a friend whose

Although a natural feeling is best for a shaded garden, it doesn't hurt to give nature a hand here and there. In a forest, remove some of the existing understory plants and prune away the lowest tree limbs. Create a meandering path through the garden and line it with plants like hostas and ferns.

mission is to collect every one of the 100 or so species, and his wooded Maine yard is a testimony to their diversity. All have very good fall color—from yellow to purple. Flowers are white or pink. Most have berries, ranging in color from yellow to rose to red to blue or black, and are very attractive to birds. Heights range from three feet to 20 feet. Some viburnums are hardier than others, but most will do well from the extreme north to the middle southern states.

With all the choices of viburnums, it is hard

to select the best for the shaded garden, but my favorite is double file (*Viburnum plicatum*), more specifically, 'Mariesii' viburnum. Its unique horizontal branching habit with white May flowers that follow along the stem is a spectacle in full bloom.

'MARIESII' can be kept in control by pruning, but plan to allow a spread of at least six to eight feet to see the full effect of its horizontal nature. My specimen does not fruit well, but the straight

Leatherleaf Viburnum

species is said to be one of the best, with very red fruit changing to black in the middle of summer. The fall color is an outstanding violet to purple, with the leaves actually mottled in both colors. Its horizontal branching is useful for the landscaper, especially to break up the vertical planes of a house. I often use 'Mariesii' viburnum as a corner accent in a design.

One of the most splendid viburnums I've seen for fall color was *V. wrightii* planted in a seashore border in Rhode Island. The shiny red clusters of berries against orange and red foliage dazzled me. An excellent smaller vibur-

num with outstanding red fall color and huge clusters of edible red berries is *V. trilobum* 'Alfredo', or compact American cranberry bush. It stays around five to six feet in height with a very upright habit. Tucked in front of its cousins, 'Alfredo' adds four-season appeal with white flowers, fall color, and fruit that hangs on for the winter birds. Another front of the border viburnum with wonderful scent is *V. carlesii*, Koreanspice viburnum. Although it attains heights of only four feet, Koreanspice has a rangy habit and is most showy when in bloom in the spring. With bright perennials in the foreground, *V. carlesii* is a good backdrop, because the flowers are semi-snowball in shape. Larger but with true snowball-shaped flowers, Chinese snowball viburnum (*V. macrocephalum*) has three- to six-inch diameter flowers on six- to eight-foot stems. Snowball viburnum does not fruit, but its flowers make the shrub well worth trying.

Some viburnums are evergreen when planted in southern climates, but maintain their deciduous habit in the north. The best example is *V. rhytidophyllum* (leatherleaf viburnum), which is distinct because of its thick, dark green, leathery, long leaves. It flowers in mid spring and will withstand deep shade.

Sculptural Interest

FOR TRUE SCULPTURAL INTEREST winter and summer, I like *Corylus avellana* 'Contorta', or Harry Lauder's walkingstick. It enjoys light shade at the front edge of shade plantings. Although botanical texts claim this shrub will reach eight to ten feet tall, it's been my experience that shade keeps it reduced in size and quite manageable. The stems twist and turn and can be distinguished even when the large three- to four-inch-long leaves are open. The flower is a male catkin that hangs like short worms from every nook and cranny of the twisted stems. The most annoying habit of Harry Lauder's walkingstick is frequent suckering of rootstock that shoots distracting straight stems skyward. As long as these stems are pruned out, the plant's effect is truly whimsical.

Rhododendrons are the old standbys of the shade garden. The genus *Rhododendron* includes deciduous azaleas. Their bright colors are fine for mass plantings as well as for individual accents to draw the eye. All of the rhododendrons and azaleas grow best as understory plants in the filtered light of trees. Both rhododendrons and azaleas prefer acidic soils (pH 4.5-6.5) and moist, woodsy conditions. The main difference between them is where the flower bud is found. Rhododendron buds are prominently displayed above the leaf whorl, and azalea buds are hidden under the bark along the branches. When pruning rhododendrons, hand-nip the spent flower heads at the top of the leaf rosette and prune the stem above the leaf whorl and bud. Azaleas may be pruned anywhere along the branches, and the bud will grow from near the cut.

R. schlippenbachii, or royal azalea, which grows in a rounded form six feet high, is an exquisite choice for the shade garden. Good red hues of fall color and fragrant, rose-colored flowers in the spring characterize this azalea, which, unfortunately, does not do well in areas with severe winters.

Flame azalea (*R. calendulaceum*) has a loose habit of growth. It derives its name from the variance in color it displays from yellows to oranges to reds. The flowers last a long time in the spring and will grow as far south as Georgia. The native *R. vaseyi*, or pink-shell azalea, is more upright at four to eight feet. Rose-colored flowers completely cover this shade lover.

Northern Azaleas

BRED FOR THE NORTHERN GARDEN, Exbury azaleas range in color from white ('White Swan') to yellow ('Sun Chariot'), pink ('Flamingo'), red ('Bullfinch') and even orange ('Gibraltar'). They flower before the leaves appear on upright four-foot stems. It's important to place 'Gibraltar' carefully into the scheme so that its garishness won't overshadow a more delicate flower like pink 'Northern Lights' azalea. Mimicking dozens of twinkling little lights, 'White Lights',

Exbury
Azalea

'Rosy Lights', 'Spicy Lights' and 'Orchid Lights' are my favorites for hardiness and compact size. 'Northern Lights' azaleas are most effective in mass plantings because the flowers of one lone plant are a little too delicate.

The evergreen varieties of rhododendrons need a northern or eastern exposure to avoid the drying winter sun and wind. Often, in northern shade gardens, it is necessary to protect the plants from the prevailing winds of winter with a wooden tepee shelter or burlap wrap. The smaller-leaved rhododendrons like 'P.J.M.' are the most hardy. 'P.J.M.' is named for Peter J. Mezitt of Weston Nurseries in

Hopkinton, Massachusetts, where the Mezitt family has produced some of the best evergreen rhododendrons for northern gardens. 'P.J.M.' has small, oval, dark green to plum-colored leaves that turn a reddish purple in the winter. It stays manageable at four to five feet tall and blooms profusely and very early with hot pink flowers. In the shade, the flowers are electric. The more subtle 'Aglow' and 'Olga Mezitt' rhododendrons have lighter rose flowers and maintain the tidy, upright but rounded habit of 'P.J.M.'. 'P.J.M.' makes a good accent combined with the green, large-leaved texture of *R. catawbiense* (Catawba rhododendron) which reaches six to ten feet in height. Catawba cultivars range in color from 'Nova Zembla' (red), 'Lee's Dark Purple', to the rose-pink of 'Roseum Elegans'. Catawba cultivars vary in hardiness, though, and should be researched before being planted in northern climates.

Equal in size to Catawba, but unique because of its deeply woolly leaf undersides, *R. smirnowii* (Smirnow rhododendron) has pink, frilly flowers. One of my favorites is the white, compact, pincushion grower with huge flowers, rhododendron 'Boule de Neige'. Its form at the front of the border is elegant and manicured. Even shorter is the dwarf rhododendron 'Purple Gem'. The leaves are small like the overall size of the plant, which only reaches 18 to 30 inches. Early spring light purple flowers add bright color to the very front of a layered planting alongside perennials and ground covers.

Broadleaf Evergreens

T HERE ARE SEVERAL other broadleaf evergreens that, like rhododendrons, enjoy the shade. Outstanding en masse at a distance as well as at a closer view is *Kalmia latifolia*, or mountain laurel. A slow grower, mountain laurel reaches heights of four to eight feet and has been hybridized to produce spring flowers from the lightest pink to deep pink with white, red or purple markings. Dwarf compact varieties have been developed as well. One reason this plant is so appealing is that the four- to six-inch flower located on the end of each branch is actually a

Mountain Laurel

clustered group of flowerlets that look like tiny shallow bowls with prominent stamens. The varieties with streaks or markings in the bowls are particularly crisp and striking.

Small and mounded, *Pieris floribunda* (mountain pieris) has fragrant white flowers that look like tiny bells on clustered long stems. Its cousin *P. japonica* (Japanese pieris) is less hardy and prefers partial shade. The flowers are similar to *P. floribunda*, but the entire plant can reach ten feet in height. Like mountain laurel, pieris blooms in the early spring.

Christmas holly look-alike *Mahonia aquifolium* (Oregon grape holly) grows three to six feet tall. The spiny leaves take on a purplish cast in winter. Yellow flowers in the spring are followed by grapelike blue-black berries that hold on into winter. Because of its short height and slow growth, *Mahonia* is a good shrub for the front of the layered shade planting.

Many broadleaf evergreens provide fine-textured foliage but don't flower in a showy way. One, a very hardy boxwood for northern lightly shaded gardens is *Buxus microphylla* var. *koreana,* or Korean boxwood. My northside garden has thriving Korean boxwoods that grow with a loose habit and stay two feet high. Resilient enough to take a constant beating of toppled snow off the roof without breakage, the foliage has that familiar boxwood scent and reminds me of my childhood in southern New England, where boxwood is a commonplace hedge or garden plant. The small, elliptical leaves hide inconspicuous flowers that attract bees with their fragrance. Common boxwood, *Buxus sempervirens* becomes very large at 15 to 20 feet tall and is much less hardy than Korean boxwood. Common boxwood is best cultivated in lightly shaded gardens where extremes of temperature are not a factor.

Ilex crenata 'Convexa' , or Japanese holly, is a hardy six- to eight-foot slow grower. The tiny leaves are concave below, forming an upside-down cup with lustrous bright green foliage. The plant has stiffly dense branches forming an upright vase shape. It is often pruned into a hedge, but in the informal shade garden will best be left alone to provide wonderful texture change. My experience with some of the so-called hardier varieties of *I. crenata*, like 'Northern Beauty', is that they die back to the snowline in northern Vermont.

For weeping habit, drooping leucothoe (*Leucothoe fontanesiana*) is the best broadleaf evergreen. It grows slowly to only three to four feet, which makes it perfect for the front of the layered shade planting where its weeping foliage touches the ground and hides leggy growth behind it while holding moisture around the stems of other plants. The white spring flowers are fragrant, but are usually hidden by the drooping foliage. Standing alone, leucothoe is also a good focal point.

Accents in the Shade Garden

WHEN PLANTED BENEATH the canopy of larger trees, a backdrop of small trees serves as a fine accent in the shade garden. A few of the maples fit this category. *Acer spicatum,* or mountain maple, grows 10 to 30 feet tall in the cool, shady, acid soil of the woods. Rounded hedge maple (*A. campestre*) will tolerate light shade and stays 25 feet in height. Amur maple (*A. ginnala*) can be grown as a multiple-stemmed shrub or pruned into a small 15-foot round-headed tree. It may not color as well in the shade, but it will vary in the fall from yellow to red. Many cultivars of amur maple have been developed for their red fruit, which is the familiar wing-shaped samara we all flew like helicopters as children.

The Japanese maple (*A. palmatum*) is the aristocrat of small shade-tolerant maples. Some, like *A. palmatum* 'Dissectum' var. *dissectum*, only grow to eight feet in height and have very finely cut leaves. Several have red leaf color throughout the growing season. In my northern Vermont shade garden, I have successfully grown *A. palmatum* 'Dissectum Atropurpureum' on the north side of the house, where its maroon leaves turn fire-engine red in the fall. For trees in this family, any location north of Massachusetts needs to be as protected as possible from damaging wind and extreme cold. My Japanese maple is surrounded by house walls on three sides and a mountain on the fourth. The shade and short growing season have kept the plant at five feet in height, but its branches spread gloriously to create a lacy umbrella of color.

Flowering Trees

Small flowering trees like *Cornus florida* (flowering dogwood) and *Cercis canadensis* (redbud) make excellent accents in the shade garden. Both do not flower reliably unless planted in moderate climates. Around 20 feet in height, flowering dogwood displays a horizontal layering effect of waves of flowers in the early spring before the green

Flowering Dogwood

leaves appear. Many cultivars have been developed for white to pink flower color, colored and variegated leaves, and abundance of bloom. Shiny red, clustered fruit ripens in the fall and hangs on into winter for the birds. A drive through the mountains of Virginia and North Carolina in the spring is unsurpassed because the understory of the woodlands seem

to be lit up with *Cornus florida*.

About the same height as flowering dogwood, redbud blooms very early in the spring in light shade. The flower buds are purple, but they turn pink when they open and last two to three weeks. In northern gardens, the buds may be nipped by the cold and fail to open.

Shade-Loving Conifers

Mixing deciduous trees with conifers is one way to break up potential monotony in a shade garden. Conifers that enjoy shade can be found in either the *Taxus* (yew) genus or the *Tsuga* (hemlock) genus. *Taxus* need a north- or east-facing exposure in the colder climates and should be protected from burning winter sun and wind. Although yews like to be pruned, the harsh shapes sometimes forced upon them are unnatural and often culturally damaging. The bottoms of the plants will die out if pruned narrower than the tops. In the shade, I prefer to let yews do their own thing, with the occasional nipping of a wayward branch. Light pruning will keep them tighter and healthier, so do keep up with it. A warning: yews are very poisonous, containing taxine in all parts of the plant except the flesh of the fruit.

Ornamentally, *Taxus* x *media* 'Densiformis', commonly known as spreading yew, is the most overused in the foundation landscape and certainly the most overpruned. It spreads wide and can grow very tall, if allowed. Its cousin, Hick's yew (*Taxus* x *media* 'Hicksii') grows upright and flat-topped. It can become 20 feet high unless pruned. Another commonly used yew, the Japanese yew or *T. cuspidata* 'Capitata' grows in a cone shape and, if left alone, can reach 40 feet tall. Called cap yew, it is often used as a corner accent in foundation planting. In the shade, its tidy habit makes a vertical statement in an otherwise wide-spreading planting.

Hemlocks grow naturally in the wooded understory and can become very tall, but with pruning can be kept at manageable heights. Cultivars have been bred that range in form from weeping and dwarf to narrowly upright. Hemlocks do not like wind, so the shaded and sheltered protection of the layered planting is ideal. The Canadian hemlock (*Tsuga canadensis*) can reach 40 feet if left unpruned. The cultivar 'Sargentii' is a weeper with exquisite broadly growing pendulous branches. As an accent plant or situated near the babbling brook in the wooded site, it will soften edges. A shaded hillside mass of sargent hemlock resembles waves of green. *T. caroliniana* (Carolina hemlock) is less hardy, equally as tall unchecked, and a slower grower than Canadian hemlock. Its texture is distinct because the needles circle the branches, creating green bottlebrushes.

Ground Cover Essentials

GROUND COVERS are a critically important element of the shade garden because they hold in the moisture around the roots of larger plants. Many woody ground covers double as vines when they hit an object or tree to which they can cling. A very adaptable ground cover/vine that tolerates heavy shade is *Euonymus fortunei* (wintercreeper). On the ground, wintercreeper rarely reaches six inches in height, but as soon as it hits a tree trunk or wall, it can climb for 50 feet or more. Wintercreeper grows fast and has many cultivars that are bred for foliage color and variegation. *E. fortunei* var. *coloratus* has dark green leaves in summer, but turns a plum-purple with red tones in the winter. *E. fortunei* 'Emerald Gaiety' sports white edges on small leaves

Virginia Creeper

that become pink margins in the winter. 'Emerald and Gold' and 'Emerald Surprise' have margins of yellow. 'Emerald Cushion' is compact and mounded.

For ground cover or vine, English ivy (*Hedera helix*) is a versatile shade lover. It is evergreen and fast-growing. My parents' house in Massachusetts had masonry buttons attached to the brick to support English ivy's holdfast roots. I have tried to grow English ivy in my Vermont shade garden with limited success, although I have seen it nearby as a lush ground cover. Obviously, a protected microclimate with good snow cover throughout the winter may be as hospitable to English ivy as Harvard Yard.

Deciduous substitutes for English ivy in colder climates are Virginia creeper (*Parthenocissus quinquefolia*) and Boston ivy (*P. tricuspidata*). Extremely vigorous to the point of being a noxious weed if not kept in check, Virginia creeper will tolerate full shade, pollution and wind. It colors to a purple-red in the fall. Boston ivy has shinier, smaller leaves but colors just as well.

Climbing hydrangea (*Hydrangea anomala petiolaris*) is an ideal vine for a north-facing wall. Long-lived fragrant white flowers arrive in late June and are borne on clinging branches that create a layered effect by branching out in many directions. Once climbing hydrangea gets established, the older stems exfoliate like birch-tree bark and are colored a rich brown.

Perennial Solutions

AN ASSORTMENT OF PERENNIAL plants and ferns is important for any shade garden. Not only do their flowers perk up low-light areas, but many have foliage with variegation or unusual size, shape and texture.

One of the most widespread groups of shade-loving perennials is, of course, the hosta, or plantain lily, genus, with over 40 species. I have miniature hostas in my rock garden, as well as giant *Hosta sieboldiana*, with its blue seersucker-textured leaves, in my shady border. A cultivar called 'Frances Williams' includes gold variegation in the leaves, while 'Northern Halo' has blue-and-cream-colored leaves. Hostas send up shoots of flowers from mid to late summer in colors of white, pink, lilac and blue. In the very front of layered plantings, along a path or along banks of a stream, the large leaves cover and soften the hard edges of rocks and pathways.

Many people grow lady's-mantle (*Alchemilla mollis*) for its flowers, but I choose it for its green-toothed and rounded leaves. Featuring a pincushion-shaped habit with yellow flowers rising from the center, *Alchemilla* is particularly interesting after it rains, when drops of water bead up on the leaves. Larger than lady's-mantle with striking dark stems and sharply toothed leaves, *Ligularia* x *prze-*

Bleeding Heart

walskii 'The Rocket' is stunning in the shade garden. 'The Rocket' sends forth 18-inch-long yellow spikes and is very easy to grow. I try to blend *Ligularia* and *Alchemilla* into the shade garden plan because even though they are outstanding in their own right, they need the foil of other plants to set them apart.

Geranium sanguineum (blood-red cranesbill) makes a good foil for *Ligularia*. Cranesbill is a three-season plant, showing profuse hot pink flowers on lush, tidy growth in the late spring with red leaf color in autumn. Although some of the cranesbills will tolerate full sun, most like a moist soil and partial shade. Complementing the deeply cut leaves of the geranium, the lacy, fine-textured foliage of *Dicentra spectabilis* (bleeding-heart) makes a delicate, old-fashioned statement in the shade garden. White or pink heart-shaped flowers hang from loose branches in the spring. *D. eximia* 'Luxuriant' is the most compact of the *Dicentra* cultivars and blooms on and off all season.

At Home with Ferns

FERNS ARE THE MOST COMMON shade-loving foliage plants. From the monster-sized ostrich fern (*Matteuccia pensylvanica*) to the delicate maidenhair fern (*Adiantum pedatum*) with its fanning shapely leaves, the ferns create backdrops and foils for brighter, showier plants like 'The Rocket'. Japanese painted fern (*Athyrium goeringianum* 'Pictum') is a gem with silver and red coloring. Hay-scented fern (*Dennstaedtia punctilobula*) not only smells like freshly cut hay when disturbed, but effectively covers a slope as a ground cover. The cinnamon fern (*Osmunda cinnamomea*) is versatile in its adaptation to sun or shade and emerges very early in the spring. Two fronds begin anew each year, one

Vinca minor

fertile and one sterile. The sticklike fertile frond turns brown after releasing its spores, then lies on the ground during the growing season while the green sterile fronds provide the background for other shade lovers. The leathery evergreen Christmas fern (*Polystichum acrostichoides*) looks like fringed feather plumes shining in the shade.

Many herbaceous ground covers have distinctive foliage characteristics too. Flowers are certainly a secondary attraction to *Ajuga reptans,* whose variety 'Burgundy Glow' is especially prolific and attractive as a prostrate grower with its red and purple leaves. Just as common as *Ajuga* in the shaded home landscape are *Pachysandra terminalis* (Japanese spurge) and *Vinca minor* (periwinkle, myrtle). My experience with both is that I have to wait a few years for full, lush growth, but once they take off, thickets of foliage cover the ground. *Vinca* has the added bonus of light blue flowers and shiny green leaves while the *Pachysandra* foliage is larger and toothed.

Lamium maculatum (spotted dead nettle) is a member of the mint family. The cultivar 'White Nancy' sparkles like polished silver in the shaded garden. One of my favorite combinations is 'White Nancy' planted with *Pulmonaria saccharata* 'Mrs. Moon'. 'Mrs. Moon' becomes eight inches in height, has pinkish-blue flowers in the early spring and remains effective in its foliage display right through to fall.

Another favorite foliage ground cover of mine is European wild ginger (*Asarum europaeum*). Shiny heart-shaped clusters of leaves hide extremely unusual tiny brown and green flowers. It spreads fast and reliably.

For completely prostrate bright green carpeting, soft as a putting green, the saginas (also known as pearlwort) Irish moss (*S. subulata*) and Scotch moss (*S. subulata* 'Aurea'), are best planted between stepping stones or featured as a soft mat in the shaded rock garden. Saginas prefer partial shade to sun, not the dense shade that a true moss tolerates, but tiny flowers and mosslike foliage are a unique texture change.

No one can resist the heady scent of lily-of-the-valley (*Convallaria majalis*). Short and spreading, lily-of-the-valley can be divided easily and transplanted. It takes a few seasons for the plants to fill in, but it is worth the wait.

Use caution when planting *Aegopodium podagraria* (bishop's weed) because a weed it is. However, when nothing else will grow, the variegated green and white leaves will cover the ground in a prolific mat. Just remember that keeping bishop's weed in check is a constant chore.

Flowers in the Shade

ONE OF MY FAVORITE GROUPS of plants bearing colorful flowers for the woodland garden are the anemones, or pasqueflowers. The most adapted to shade conditions is *Anemone sylvestris* 'Snowdrops'. Large, pure white flowers top 18-inch stems in

Foxglove

the late spring. *Fritillaria meleagris*, or snake's-head lily, comes in colors that range from dark red to maroon, purple, white and yellow. The plants stay short, at about a foot, and bloom early in the spring. Equally showy but later to bloom is *Astilbe*. Given partial shade and lots of fertilizer, it grows quickly and profusely. The flower plumes come in white, pink and red. Mass astilbes for best effect, because the thin flower plumes beg for company. I like *A. tacquetii* 'Superba' because it blooms off and on all summer.

A shade garden can be perked up in the late fall, at Christmastime or very early spring (depending on the climate) with the Christmas rose (*Helleborus niger*). The three-inch white flowers are borne on 12-inch stems. Its cousin, the Lenten rose (*H. orientalis*) is easier to grow, a little taller, but less hardy.

Primulas make up a large genus of perennials that like partial shade and wet soils. They vary in appearance, but all bloom in the spring. The leaves are crinkly, long and formed like a rosette around the base. *Primula vulgaris*, the English primrose, only reaches six inches in height and blooms in a rainbow of colors. My favorite is *P. denticulata*, which forms a golf-ball-shaped group of flowerlets in pastel shades of pink, white and cream.

Another old-fashioned shade garden must is the violet. Violets can be just as much of a nuisance as bishop's weed, because of their spreading habit, but the appealing heart-shaped leaves and butterfly-shaped flowers make the trouble worthwhile. *Viola odorata* (sweet violet) possesses the violet color and sweetly scented flower associated with a heady stroll on an early summer evening along a wooded path.

One of my favorite choices by far for the partially shaded garden is foxglove (*Digitalis* x *mertonensis*), however my luck in keeping it happy and thriving in Vermont has been marginal. The plant is biennial, but should reseed well enough to provide a continuity of growth from year to year. Its cousin, *D. grandiflora*, seems to be more reliable, however the yellow flowers don't have the appeal for me of those of *D.* x *mertonensis*.

For real height in the rear of the shaded border, there are several choices. *Aruncus dioicus* (goatsbeard) can reach four to six feet, shooting cream-colored clusters of flowers similar to astilbes, only larger. In the same family, *Filipendula ulmaria*, or queen-of-the-meadow, can be as tall as *Aruncus*, but sends feathery, plumelike white flowers on naked stems . Even spikier in flower and taller at six feet is the white *Cimicifuga racemosa*, also known as black snakeroot. Several *Cimicifuga* planted together are a great backdrop in the middle of the summer when they are blooming.

Annual Appeal

BECAUSE OF THE LIMITED possibilities for a great variety of flower color among shade-loving perennials, consider adding sharpness and distinction through the use of annual plants. Tuberous begonias offer the shade gardener numerous intense colors in yellow, reds, white and pink. The flowers are fancier and more petaled than regular begonias and are perfect for hanging baskets in the shade as well as for window boxes and gardens. Tuberous begonias can be dug up in the fall and replanted in the spring.

Another common annual is coleus, which is grown for its remarkable variety of foliage colors. Many of the leaves are soft to the touch and harbor as many as three or four colors within the same leaf. Placed among pastels and white-flowering perennials and shrubs like bleeding heart and viburnum, coleus offers a constant source of flash and color. Equally colorful in leaf, but somewhat less garish, caladiums have very large heart-shaped leaves in varying combinations of white, green, pink, silver and red. The color tends to settle in and around the veins of the leaves and radiates to the margins. The 12-inch-high tropical looking plants make a lush accent in the front of the border.

Whatever plants you choose for that shady area of your property, don't be afraid to express your tastes and moods in color and texture. Experiment regularly with combinations or partnering of plants that complement each other. The versatility of perennials allows for easy transplanting in most cases, so this season's disappointment can be transformed into next year's splendor.

Chapter Eight

Walkways & Patios

Smoothing the rough edges

WHY, I WONDER, is the world so full of bland, squared-off wooden decks that look every bit like the afterthought they were? What drives homeowners to install brick walkways that become so chipped, cracked and bumpy that traversing their length is a major athletic feat for anyone who is not young and light-footed? Is there some mischievous law of physics dictating that the smooth surface of every newly installed stone patio become an obstacle course of puddles, rough edges and bumps within a single season?

Little wonder that so many homeowners abandon dreams of quaintness and settle for the mundane but oh-so-practical virtues of poured concrete and pressure-treated two-by-fours—to the point of overkill.

I get great pleasure from removing concrete walks and wooden decks to make way for properly installed pavers and natural stone. And even more pleasure when I return to the same site years later and find the patio as smooth and level as it was the day I left the job site; the walkway as safe and practical as it is aesthetic.

In the world of dry-laid walkways and patios, it is entirely possible to have your cake and eat it too. You can build something as practical as it is visually appealing. The key is proper construction. A well-built walkway or patio made of the right materials should last a lifetime.

*If you find yourself in a position to replace an old wooden deck,
don't feel obligated to replicate the original, mistakes and all, particularly if the
existing structure is a traditional squared-off raised deck.*

Problem

Unimaginative & Poorly Placed Wooden Decks

THE SAD FACT is that most wooden decks I've seen are built without any care taken to analyze the way the space will be used or what size the deck should be in relation to the house and yard. So if you find yourself in the position of having to replace an old deck, don't feel compelled to replicate the original, mistakes and all. Whatever you do, don't feel locked into the traditional squared-off raised deck out of the sliding door with several steps to the ground. Square and rectangular decks have unusable corners, and raised decks breed junk and weeds in the space beneath.

Remedy

A Well-Designed Patio

GROUND-LEVEL PATIOS, whatever the surface material, are a fine alternative to raised wooden decks. Obviously, the first decision to be made is where to locate the new patio. A sunny exposure is best, but if the house is oriented with the backyard to the east or north, pulling the patio away from the house to catch what sun there is will enhance its usefulness.

First and foremost, remember that a patio is outdoor living space, an extension of the living room, dining room or enclosed porch. Determining how the space will be used will help you settle on size. Be sure to leave enough room for items such as barbecues, dining tables

*Ground-level patios, whatever the surface material,
are fine alternatives to raised wooden decks. The angular lines of a home can be
softened by ovals or free-form curves, which also provide more usable space.*

and chairs and chaise lounges. Sometimes, it is helpful to make scaled cut-outs of the furniture and fit them into a layout on paper. Keep in mind how many people are usually accommodated when entertaining. Finally, don't hesitate to break up the space by creating more than one level, especially if egress from the house requires more than one step down. The transition can graduate from upper to ground level, with landings large enough for dining, grilling or sunbathing.

Don't be confined by straight edges. The angular lines of a home can be softened by oval or free-form curves, and all the space is useful when the patio is void of unusable, empty corners. Flexible edging and paving materials allow creation of pleasantly serpentine lines.

If stone or brick is a part of the facade of the home or there are other features already exist-

ing in the yard made out of a certain material, it may look best to match what is already there. If the material can't be matched exactly, it's probably better to introduce a completely different look.

The house's architectural style, the size of the lot, and whether or not it is in a city or rural setting will dictate whether the patio should be formal or informal. If the area where the patio will be built is in the rear of the house, it can be more relaxed than if it is in the front. A free-form patio will lend a casual feel to the space, particularly if the patio has bluestone or fieldstone as a surface. A patio of brick or precast-concrete pavers will be more formal, especially if laid in a pattern like herringbone or basket weave. A plain running-bond pattern, where the bricks are placed end to end, is casual, but can be dressed up with

133

contrasting edging in a different color, size or configuration.

I prefer to leave spaces for plants wherever possible to cool and soften the hard surfaces of patios. Leaving a shapely cut-out in the patio for a tree will provide relief from harsh sunlight. Trellises, pergolas and awnings are good choices for patio shading too. Planter boxes, either built into the patio or sitting on top of it, will give a sense of enclosure, lending privacy and division to a busy yard.

Problem
Gaps & Grass

UNWANTED GRASS-FILLED GAPS between patio and walkway pavers develop over time and for several reasons. Grass growing between pavers can be the product of nonsterile (containing weed seeds) backfill. Wide gaps usually occur when the edging has been forced out of place because of lateral pressure from compaction—or if no edging was used at all. Weed seeds fall in waiting cracks to create a perennial problem requiring painstaking hand weeding or applications of herbicide.

Remedy
A Proper Fit

SEVERAL TYPES OF EDGING can ensure that pavers fit together properly, but the paving material dictates which type should be used. If the patio or walkway is one level, I prefer the least obtrusive edging, focusing attention, instead, on the patio surface. The best edging for this effect is installed be-

low the surface (actually ending three-eighths of an inch below the top of the paver) so it isn't seen at all. It is black PVC, flexible or rigid, depending on the shape of the area, and it can only be used with brick or precast-concrete pavers.

If the surface is bluestone or another regularly sized thin stone like slate, the best edging choice is aluminum. It is installed with its surface pressed against the side of the stone, flush with the top but barely visible because it is only one-eighth-inch thick. (For straight edges, order the aluminum a little thicker, which is less bendable.) It is available in silver or black.

Wood and PVC plastic with rolled pipe-like flanges have been overused as edgers. I

have also learned to avoid using wooden boards as an edging material. They always heave, and the resulting unsightliness detracts from the patio material. However, if the patio is bilevel or needs steps, I would consider six-by-six timbers as edging because they are economical and effectively provide the riser needed for stairs.

Granite, which is often used for curbing of sidewalks and streets in cities, is a more aesthetic choice than timber. Quarries custom-cut pieces in positive and inverse curves as well as in straight sections. They will also fire the stepping surface to roughen it so it won't be

Gaps in walkways, **facing page,** *occur when the edging is forced out of place or no edging is used at all. Proper edging assures that pavers stay together. The least obtrusive edging for brick or concrete pavers is black PVC, which is installed just below the surface,* **inset,** *and is virtually invisible once the backfill has been added.*

slippery. The granite usually comes at least three to four inches thick, and the supplier will advise how long the segments need to be. Obviously, several pieces must be placed side by side to go a distance, because one long piece would not be transportable. With granite, it is necessary to caulk the joints completely to avoid seepage of the base material through the gaps.

Problem

Bad Stone & Old Brick

I ONCE INSTALLED A WALKWAY twice inside of one year because the first stones shattered after a single winter. If stone is used that splits too easily or brick is used that is not fired specifically for outdoor paving, shattering will always result.

Remedy

Choose a Durable Surface

SURFACING MATERIALS must be thoroughly researched, especially if they are natural. I have found it a wise practice not to use any natural-surface material unless it has stood the test of time, at least one year, in previous installations in my immediate area. Precast-concrete pavers are a very practical and durable alternative to brick and natural stone for walkways and patios. In fact, they are so sturdy that many homeowners are opting for paver driveways rather than asphalt or concrete.

Concrete pavers are manufactured in such a way that there is little or no space between the pavers when they are installed properly. They are available in styles that are shaped to allow round and curving pathways, as well as straight. For the traditionalist, there are concrete pavers that imitate brick in colors ranging from clay red to gray, with mottled blends in between.

Natural stones like bluestone, slate and fieldstone, while not as durable as concrete, can also make fine surfaces for walkways and patios. Bluestone and slate can be cut with a saw to create curved edges, so any shape is possible. An informal fieldstone patio blends well with the environment, especially when indigenous stone is used. But fieldstone is not the most practical surface for shoveling snow on a front walkway.

Problem
Peaks & Valleys

WALKWAYS WITH A MIDDLE HUMP or so many bumps, pockets and holes that guests and family members alike literally trip down their length may look quaint, but are totally impractical. Usually, the cause for bumps and valleys lies with improper or nonexistent base preparation. A poorly graded rolling base will mirror itself on the surface after a single winter of freezing and thawing, settling and heaving. No matter what the climate, if the base is not graded well or is prepared with unsuitable drainage material, there will be a poor result.

Precast-concrete pavers are a practical and durable alternative to brick or natural stone as surface material for walkways and patios. They are available in styles that allow for rounded and curving edges, as well as straight.

Natural stone, such as bluestone, while not as durable as concrete, can also make a fine surface for walkways and patios. Bluestone can be cut to form any shape desired, including both curved and straight edges. It also makes fine treads for the steps leading to the patio.

Remedy
A Smooth Start

INSTALLATION TECHNIQUES for patios and walkways vary somewhat from surface material to surface material, but there are some basics that remain constant.

If lighting is part of the scheme, be sure to install wire and/or conduit under the drainage gravel before the installation is complete in order to maximize lighting options on all sides of the walkway or patio.

When using brick or precast-concrete pavers, excavate a foot of soil, making the space six to eight inches wider than the finished size. That extra width will ensure that the edging material used will not heave during freeze/thaw cycles. The one-foot depth will bring the surface of the patio up to the desired level after the addition of gravel, sand and the pavers. Use a transit to determine where water will flow, and grade the base appropriately. It is critical to maintain the proper grade through every step of the installation.

Next, backfill with approximately nine inches of clean gravel, compacting several times with a plate compactor. It is absolutely essential to "screed," or smooth, the subsurface after it is compacted. To do so, use three 2x4 pieces of wood, one cut to the exact width of the walkway (called the screed board) or to a manageable length for a patio. The other two 2x4s (rails) can be any length. They are buried in the subsurface gravel parallel to each other so that the two-inch edge is seen flush to the gravel. The ends closest to the house should be highest and drop away one inch every eight feet to maintain the correct pitch for drainage. Kneel between the buried rails, lay the screed board across them, and drag it towards your body scraping it for the length of the rails. When that surface area is smooth, add more base material as needed to maintain the depth and pitch, compact again, and screed a second time. Remove the rails, fill in the holes left behind by the rails, tamp the filled in area with a hand tamper, and move the rails to the next unscreeded area. Repeat until the entire patio or walkway has been done.

WHEN THE SUBSURFACE is completely screeded and compacted, discard the rails and use one inch diameter PVC pipes laid on top of the subsurface in the same position as the wooden rails. Since the subsurface has perfect pitch, it is not necessary to keep measuring, only to keep the bedding material one inch deep. The one inch PVC pipes will do a satisfactory job of that.

Put about an inch of sand on top of the gravel subsurface and compact. Drag the screed board towards you along the pipes, compact again, and add sand to maintain the one inch depth. Screed and compact a second time. Remove the pipes, fill in the gaps left behind, tamp with a hand tamper, and move the pipes to the next area until the entire surface is a perfectly smooth one inch depth ready to have bricks or pavers laid on top of it.

Lay the pavers or bricks, keeping the joints as tight as possible. Leave out pavers where they need to be cut. Install the edging and fit

in any cut pavers. Spread dry sand on top. For brick installations, sweep the sand into the joints. For concrete-paver installations, run the plate compactor over top of them to vibrate the sand into the joints.

Bluestone, slate or other flat natural stones follow a similar installation regimen.

However, when using bluestone or slate, rockfines, not sand, are the preferred bedding material. Because bluestone and slate are natural, their thicknesses may vary, so it is necessary to level each stone with the next.

Fieldstone can be laid in a formal manner using the same initial procedures as with bricks and bluestone. Grade the base and backfill, and compact as usual, but measure the average thickness of the fieldstone before finishing the compaction and backfill procedures, because the fieldstone, being a natural product, has varying thicknesses. The final rockfine base material should be leveled as usual, but will be dug out to accommodate each individual stone. There is no need for edging if the stone is at least three inches thick. Leave an irregular edge for natural results, and sweep rockfines into the joints. Finally, backfill the edges with soil.

For informality, fieldstone or bluestone and slate can be laid with space left for soil and grass or ground covers in between. Lay the

To achieve a more informal effect, fieldstone can be laid with space left for soil and grass or other ground covers such as creeping thyme, **above.**

stone out on the ground. Cut through the turf around the individual stones using the stone as a template. Dig out the space and backfill with gravel, compact with a hand tamper, and level the stones as you go, maintaining the pitch.

Building a walkway or patio sounds like a lot of hard work, but if properly done, the results should give a lifetime of satisfaction.

Sources

Loran, Inc.
1705 East Colton Ave.
Redlands, CA 92374
(714) 794-2121
The original low-voltage landscape lighting, "Nightscaping" stresses the light and the effect it creates, not the source of the light. The fixtures are subtle and inobtrusive but shed as much light as any conventional fixtures. Easy to install.

Uni Paving Group USA
4362 North Lake Blvd.
Palm Beach Gardens, FL 33410
(407) 626-4666
Manufacturers of precast-concrete pavers. If you contact the above address, they will provide information about dealers in your area.

Ideal Concrete Block Co.
232 Lexington St.
Waltham, MA 02254
(617) 894-3200
Manufacturer and distributor of the highly regarded "Pisa" concrete-wall systems.

Saratoga Rail Fence & Supply, Inc.
P.O. Box 13864
Albany, NY 12212-9600
(800) 869-8703
PVC fencing, a no-maintenance alternative to post and rail.

Jerith Manufacturing Co.
3901 G St.
Philadelphia, PA 19124
(800) 344-2242
Delgard Aluminum Ornamental Fencing
8600 River Road
Delair, NJ 08110
(800) 235-0185
Two sources for aluminum fencing. Both offer several design choices, sizes, gate styles and color brochures.

Eastern International, Inc.
274 Middle Island Rd.
Medford, NY 11763
(800)-FENCE-88
Cedar Mix and Match fencing as well as many other styles, wooden and otherwise, are offered by this distributor. Most fencing is delivered by common carrier, so be sure to ask about delivery pricing when ordering.

Permaloc
13505 Barry Street
Holland, MI 49424
(800) 356-9660
A reliable source for aluminum edging, in either polished silver, black anodized or black duraflex. The black is less visible in the landscape.

Pave Edge, Inc.
P.O. Box 31126
Bloomington, MN 55431
(800) 728-3832
Below-ground PVC edge restraints are the specialty of this manufacturer/distributor. Designed for use with precast-concrete pavers and brick.

Waterford Gardens
74 East Allendale Road
Saddle River, NJ 07458
(201) 327-0721
For water gardening equipment, plants, fish, and pond supplies, this mail-order catalog is beautifully illustrated and chock full of advice.

Lilypons Water Gardens
P.O. Box 10
6800 Lilypons Road
Buckeystown, MD 21717-0010
(800) 999-5459
Features all the supplies needed for successful water gardening.

Country Wetlands Nursery
S75 W20755 Field Drive
Muskego, WI 53150
(414) 679-1268
Specialties include wetland, prairie and woodland plants and seeds.

Banyai Hostas
11 Gates Circle
Hockessin, DE 19707
(302) 239-0887
Banyai's, the second-oldest hosta nursery in the country, grows as many as two hundred hosta cultivars and species.

Fancy Fronds
1911 4th Avenue West
Seattle, WA 98119
(206) 483-0205
A major grower of temperate climate ferns, this company propagates only from spores and is adamant about not collecting from the wild. They specialize in Victorian-era cultivars and also introduce new ferns from Asia and South America.

Gilbert H. Wild & Son, Inc.
P.O. Box 338
Sarcoxie, MO 64862-0338
(417) 548-3514
The lover of daylilies will enjoy the colorful photos offered by this mail-order grower.

Siskiyou Rare Plant Nursery
2825 Cummings Road
Medford, OR 97501
(503) 772-6846
For the best and unique in alpine perennials, Siskiyou is a respected and well-known source. The experienced gardener as well as the novice will enjoy their catalog.

Porterhowse Farms
41370 Southeast Thomas Road
Sandy, OR 97055
(503) 668-5834
This 13-year-old mail-order retail nursery grows several hundred species of conifers, specializing in the dwarf and rare. Porterhowse also grows rock-garden alpines, including over 500 varieties of sempervivum and at least 80 sedum varieties.

Further Reading

Water Gardens
Peter Stadelmann
Barron's Educational Series, Inc.
Hauppauge, NY
A good mix of technical advice and diagrams with exceptional photos of natural ponds, streams and man-made water features. Fish, plant and maintenance information is included.

The Atlas of Garden Ponds
Herbert R. Axelrod, et al.
TFH Publications, Neptune, NJ
Beautifully illustrated bible of pond design and construction, including information on planting and fish care.

Manual of Woody Landscape Plants
Michael A. Dirr
Stipes Publishing Company
Champaign, IL
In its fourth edition, the "Manual" is known to horticultural students all over the country.

Perennials for Your Garden
Alan Bloom
Floraprint U.S.A., Chicago, IL
Color photographs of the major perennials with descriptive text.

Alpines for Your Garden
Alan Bloom
Floraprint U.S.A., Chicago, IL
The guide to short perennials at home in a rock garden and the front of a border. Well illustrated.

Taylor's Guide to Perennials
*Taylor's Guide to Ground Covers,
   Vines & Grasses*
Taylor's Guide to Shrubs
Taylor's Guide to Shade Gardening
Norman Taylor
Houghton Mifflin Company
Boston, MA
These little guides are very complete and helpful when a reliable reference is needed.

The Rodale Book of Composting
Deborah L. Martin and
Grace Gershuny, Eds.
Rodale Press, Emmaus, PA
This book runs the gamut from history to methodology and from the smallest of cinder-block-and-wire bins to the most elaborate wooden rodent-proof composter.

The Hosta Book
Paul Aden
Timber Press, Portland, OR
Inclusive and highly readable book covering cultivation, pests, species and companion plants for the woodland garden.

Daylilies:
Lewis and Nancy Hill
Storey Communications, Inc.
Pownal, VT
The Hills have 40 years of experience growing daylilies.

*Cox's Guide to Choosing
Rhododendrons*
Peter and Kenneth Cox
Timber Press, Portland, OR
Systematic listing composed by owners of a family business located near Perth, Scotland. An extremely detailed account.

The Harrowsmith Perennial Garden
Patrick Lima
Camden House Publishing Ltd.
Camden East, Ontario
A truly reliable guide for northern and cold-climate gardeners.

The Backyard Book
Tricia Foley, Consulting Editor
Text by Rachel Carley
Viking Penguin, Inc., New York, NY
Inspirational photographs prompt even the least creative mind and the most inexperienced designer. When I am stuck for an idea, this is the book to which I turn.

Garden Paths
Gordon Hayward
Camden House Publishing Inc.
Charlotte, VT
Line drawings illustrate patterns and ideas as well as construction techniques. Color photographs from sites around the world celebrate the diversity of pathways.

*Know Your Garden Series:
   Ornamental Conifers*
Julie Grace, General Editor
Timber Press, Portland, OR
For the connoisseur as well as the home gardener, this complete reference lists the diverse conifer group using friendly descriptions and informative photographs that emphasize the attributes of the conifers and clearly distinguish their individual qualities.

Conifers
J.R. Van Hoey Smith and
D.M. Van Gelderen
Timber Press, Beaverton, OR
This well-respected volume is the authority on the subject. Horticulturists swear by the detailed description and the accuracy of the color plates.

Andersen Source List
Horticultural Library
University of Minnesota
Minnesota Landscape Arboretum
Chanhassen, MN
A wealth of information for those seeking the source of a certain plant. All nurseries included in the list will ship plant material. Both wholesale and retail nurseries are included, from the very large and well-known to mom-and-pop operations. Common names are provided for those unfamiliar with the botanical counterparts.

Index